REAL WEALTH *by investing in* REAL ESTATE

RALPH R. ROBERTS
WITH
JOE HAFNER

Library of Congress Cataloging-in-Publication Data

Roberts, Ralph.
Real wealth through real estate / Ralph Roberts and Joe Hafner.
p. cm.
Includes index.
ISBN 0-7352-0235-4
1. Real estate investment. 2. Real estate investment—United States. I. Title.

HD1382.5 .R6226 2001
332.63'24—dc21 2001021570

Associate Publisher: *Ellen Schneid Coleman*
Production Editor: *Mariann Hutlak*
Page Design/Composition: *Robyn Beckerman*

This publication is designed to provide accurate and authoritative information in regard to the subject matter covered. It is sold with the understanding that the publisher is not engaged in rendering legal, accounting, or other professional service. If legal advice or other expert assistance is required, the services of a competent professional person should be sought.

—*From the Declaration of Principles jointly adopted by a Committee of the American Bar Association and a Committee of Publishers and Associations.*

Printed in the United States of America

10 9 8 7 6 5 4 3 2 1

ISBN 0-7352-0235-4

Paramus, NJ 07652

http://www.phdirect.com

This book is dedicated to my accounting gurus,
Joe Sirianni and Rhonda Murdoch.
Without your systems and solutions,
I would not be nearly as successful as I am today.

CONTENTS

ACKNOWLEDGMENTS

First and foremost, I will recognize the incredible efforts and talents of my co-author, Joe Hafner, who has through the years been a valued business associate, consultant, advisor, and friend. Since he first got me into *TIME* magazine, Joe has played a vital role in my success. His writing and editing skills are unmatched and, as I watch his success grow in Tennessee, it's obvious that he knows a little bit about real estate, too.

Thank you to my agent, Jeff Herman, who put this whole deal together; to associate editor Ellen Schneid Coleman and production editor Mariann Hutlak at Prentice Hall Direct, whose dedication and close attention to detail made this book immeasurably better; to my family, Kathleen, Kolleen, Kyle, Kaleigh, and Spikette, for their infinite patience, understanding, and advice during the writing and editing process; to my whole staff at 30521 Schoenherr, for keeping the operation running smoothly; and to all of my customers—past, present, and future—who have allowed me the honor of helping them with their real estate needs.

Finally, there is an additional group of people I want to recognize by name. These individuals have all directly or indirectly played a key role in the creation of this book:

Peter Allen
Lance Avery
Sue Bernier
Ralph Bianchi
Howard Brinton
Paul Corona
Dave Ebner
Cherie Eilertsen
John Fenn
Chuck Ferarolis
Tony Ferris
Marge Fraser
John Gallagher
Victor Gamba
Hugo Garofalo
Ken Haggard
Don Houser
Richard Ian

John Jacobs
Harry Kalogerakos
Mike Keracher
Sophie Landa
Patrick Liew
Sasha Martin
Dick Mazur
Eleanor Alcala Mercier
Sherry & Scott Mullins
Rhonda Murdoch
Rose Orlando
Mark Paczkowski
Ed Page
Frank Palazzolo
Robert Pante
Melisa Patterson
Eddy Peters
Lou Peters
Roger Petri
Alex Rehahn
Monica Reynolds
DW Roberts
Frank Sattler
Bill Scarborough
Tim Schawn
Peter Schneiderman
Joe Sirianni
Pat Skiles
Frank Stewart
Greg Sugg
Steve Tarczy
John Thornton
Betty Tomczak
Maryann Tomczak
Bob Van Goethem
Dennis Waitley
Raymond Wang

What this book can do for you

I've traveled all over the world teaching real estate professionals how to sell more houses. Some of them have even come to my offices in Warren, Michigan, to spend the day with my staff and me in an attempt to increase their production. The thing that always amazes me about the thousands of people with whom I've discussed real estate over the last 25 years is that the majority of them believe the way to get rich in real estate is to be an agent who puts deals together for other people. Don't get me wrong. You can make a good living helping other people buy and sell their homes. In fact, I've done very well as a real estate agent myself.

Unfortunately, those who focus on that and only that aspect of real estate are missing the real path to wealth in real estate. To achieve real wealth in the real estate industry, you have to invest in property yourself. Many people—myself included—have made millions of dollars doing exactly that. The fact that you're reading this book suggests to me that you understand this concept. If that's the case, you're off to a very good start.

The truth of the matter is that you CAN get rich investing in real estate. But, unlike what the late-night TV real estate gurus might tell you, it probably won't happen overnight, and you probably *will* have to roll up your sleeves and do some work. The good news is that it can be done by just about anyone who is armed with a plan and a bit of know-how. That's why I've written this book—I'll provide you with the plan and the know-how. From there, you'll be ready to do the work.

I knew I wanted to be involved in real estate in some way since I was a small child watching my dad, who was a builder, putting up subdivisions in and around metro Detroit. In fact, I first tried my hand in real estate as an investor—not as an agent. When I graduated from high school at age 18, I took the money I received as graduation gifts and used it as a down payment on a house. I paid my mortgage by renting out rooms to my friends on a weekly basis. Eventually, I even rented out my own room and slept in the hallway. Not long after that, I bought my second house and I was on my way in real estate investment. Being a landlord and investor has played a significant role in my business ever since.

There's no reason why you can't do exactly like I did. (Although you may not want to rent out your own room!) And although it doesn't hurt to have some knowledge of the real estate industry, you don't need to be an expert to get started. After all, I got things going as a 19-year-old kid who had been voted "Most Likely *NOT* to Succeed" in high school. So, if I can do it, you can certainly do it, too.

One thing I do want to emphasize before getting into the how-to of real estate investing is that I will be offering only general guidelines and concepts based on my 20-plus years of personal experience investing in real estate. There are no hard and fast rules, and local laws can vary dramatically from place to place. That is why I urge you to learn your local laws and make friends with real estate professionals, attorneys, and government officials in your area who can give some insight into the unique aspects of your marketplace.

Before you start investing, come up with a plan. Do you want to focus mainly on acquiring rental properties? Or are "flippers" more to your liking? Perhaps you'll choose some combination of the two. Which methods of acquisition best fit your personality and skills? How many properties do you want to buy each year? Will you use your own money or somebody else's cash? Are you handy yourself or will you have to assemble a list of quality contractors and craftsmen to do work for you? And as you get started, always remember to exercise caution. Don't lose sight of the fact that, while you can make a lot of money (you can even become a millionaire!) using the ideas in this book, a single careless mistake could be financially devastating.

The point is, don't be a bull in a china shop. Organize your thoughts and set some goals before you rush forward—the stakes are too high not to. But above all, find enjoyment in what you do. Just think—you're doing something that can allow you to achieve financial freedom. Finally, don't be intimidated by the process or by doomsayers who tell you that you don't have what it takes or that you don't know what you're doing. These are probably people who just don't have the drive or courage to go out and make it happen for themselves.

Based on my many years of experience and the satisfying real estate career I've built for myself, I've laid out my knowledge and advice in this book. The tools for your success are all right here. Now, it's all up to you. Go grab that brass ring.

Ralph Roberts

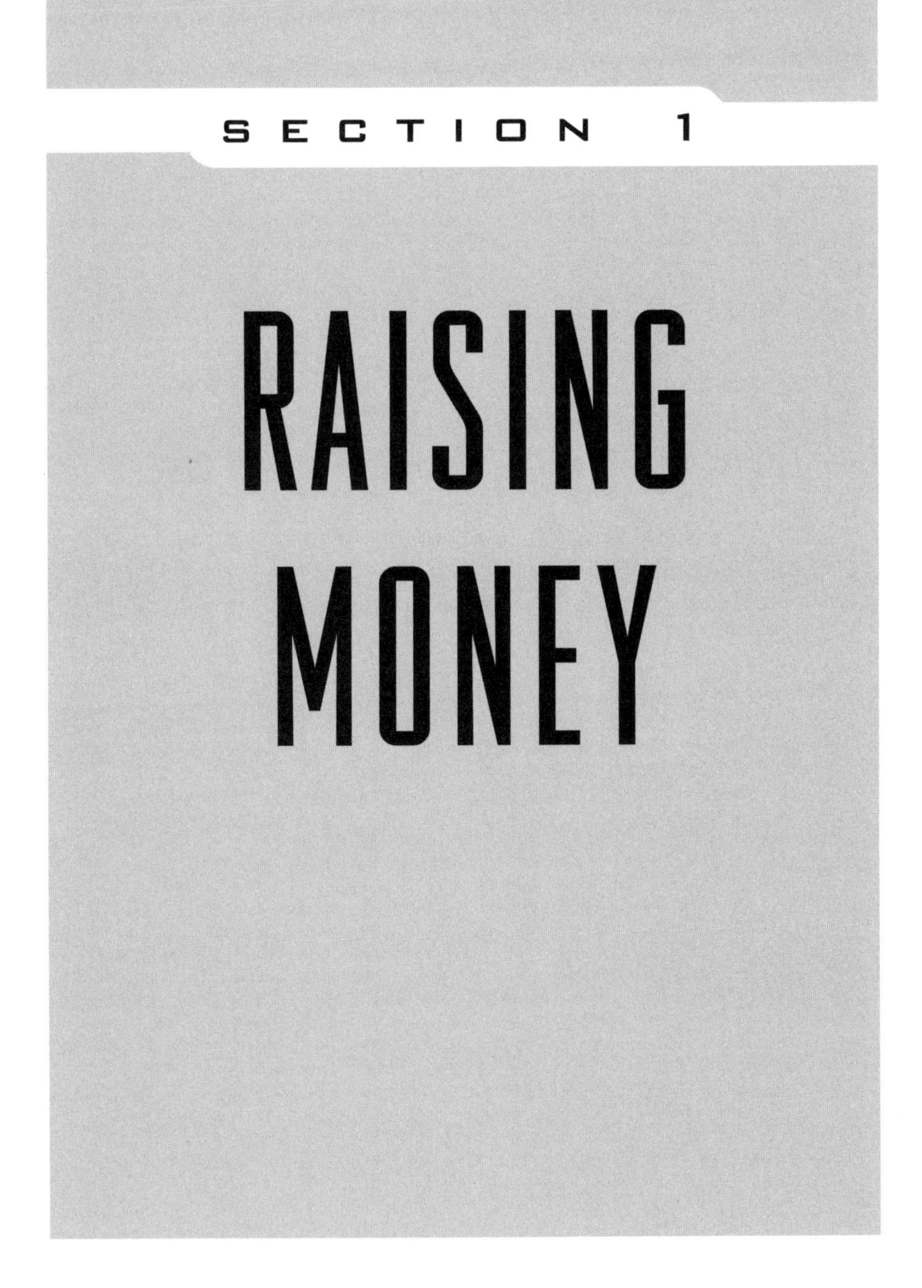

SECTION 1

RAISING MONEY

CHAPTER 1

You *Usually* Need Access to Money to Make Money

Okay, you know that you can make a ton of money investing in real estate. But how do you get started? Well, first of all, you're going to need some money. I say some money, but actually you're most likely going to need quite a bit of money.

So where will you get it? You may be fortunate enough to have 20 or 30 thousand or more dollars sitting in a bank or brokerage account. But what if, like many Americans, you're basically living paycheck to paycheck, barely paying your bills with little or no investment capital or disposable income?

Tapping your financial resources

If you're one step away from the poorhouse, you may be able to supply yourself with more money than you think. And even if you're the second coming of Daddy Warbucks, it may still be in your best interests to use someone else's capital for your real estate investing. One of the places I first went for money was the bank of Julia Rowland—my mom's mother. My grandmother, who was also one of the first people to introduce me to sales, had some money of her own and used it to help me get started in real estate. When I found an investment property worth buying, she would write me a check. The great thing about the bank of Julia Rowland was that I never paid interest on the funds I borrowed. Even though I tried, she would never accept it. Even now, I still use other people's money as much as possible when I'm buying property, even though I usually do have to pay interest. Perhaps my early positive experience with my grandmother has played a role in the positive way I look at borrowing capital.

How much money will you need?

When it comes to money issues, I want to make sure that you don't have any misconceptions. I'm sure that you've seen the late-night-TV real estate gurus who claim you can get rich investing in no-money-down properties. The fact is that although there are no-money-down deals out there, they are few and far between. And, those kinds of deals usually present themselves to people who are active in the marketplace. In any case, it's highly unlikely that your first deal will be of the no-money-down variety. So getting some money together has to be a top priority.

The next question, of course, is: How much money will you need?

There is no easy answer to this question. It depends upon several factors. Are you looking to ease into real estate investment slowly or make it a full-time business? Do you want to work on one house at a time or buy up everything you can find that looks like a solid deal?

You can get started with access to as little as five or ten thousand dollars. But, even if you want to go after a single property at a time, it will be much easier to get started if you can get your hands on 40 or 50 thousand dollars. And, if like most people, you don't have that kind of money at your disposal, you'll have to find investors.

Attracting investors

But why would other people give you their money? Well, they won't actually give it to you—unless you happen to have a rich, generous relative. Investors will put up the capital because they expect to make some sort of return on their money. To get access to this cash, you'll have to convince potential investors that you have the know-how to profit from real estate investing. (This will be examined in depth in Chapter 3.)

Once you have some confidence and a few transactions under your belt, the sky's the limit. After you know what you're doing, credit limits of a million dollars or more aren't out of the question. And guess what? There are people and institutions with that kind of money available for these kinds of ventures. They want to lend it to someone. Why shouldn't they lend it to you? But I'm getting ahead of myself. We have to start with baby steps.

Summary

You can get started in real estate investing even if you don't have much money of your own. You can tap financial sources that range from your dear old Aunt Betty to your local banking institution. Of course, you may feel most comfortable spending only what you already have. I'll talk more about the best ways to invest with your own money in the next chapter.

CHAPTER 2

Using Your Own Money to Invest in Real Estate

Sherry Mullins is a real estate agent who has worked with me for more than 13 years. The first time I met her was when she came to me with her husband, Scott, to get my help in buying a home. She was a housewife with an interior decorating business on the side and no practical real estate experience. I helped Sherry and Scott buy a modest 1,000-square-foot ranch. They paid a little below market value because the house was in need of some work. Sherry and Scott were handy enough to do the work themselves, and in no time at all they had a nice lump of equity in their home, even though they put very little money down.

Building wealth one property at time

Like most people, the Mullinses would have been perfectly happy to stay in this house for a few years, build up their equity and then maybe move to a bigger home, but Sherry had me dogging her to move up to another property as quickly as possible. So over the next ten years, Sherry and her family would live for a few months (sometimes a year or two) in what was virtually a construction site as they fixed up the home they were living in. Once the project was completed, I would come along and talk them into buying another home. They would either sell the one they had just finished or turn it into a rental property. They bought houses through foreclosure and tax auctions, homes in need of TLC that were listed on our Multiple Listing Service, and properties from me that I had bought for cash from people who for various reasons wanted or needed to sell their homes quickly.

After more than a decade of this type of activity, the Mullinses had significantly raised their net worth, acquired several income-producing rental properties, and were living in their dream house—a large four-bedroom place out in the country. In the Mullinses' case, an additional benefit came in the form of Sherry's new career with my company, a result of her realization that she had a talent for the real estate business.

The point of this story is that Sherry and Scott basically built all of their real estate wealth with their own money—and they didn't start out with a fortune either. Sure, they got some financing from mortgage lenders and, in some cases, from the sellers themselves. (We'll get into seller financing later on.) But the key for them was that they made a commitment to build their wealth over time by investing their own sweat and money. It wasn't always easy, but they developed a plan and stuck to it.

The good news was that as they accumulated properties and made profits on sales, there were no investors to pay off. Of course, it took them much longer to really profit from their activities than it would have if they had had access to extra money, because then they would have been able to acquire income-producing properties more quickly and hire other people to do the repairs.

The pros and cons of using your own money

As you put together your own real estate investment plan, you'll have to make some choices. If you decide mainly to use your own money, here are some of the benefits and challenges you should anticipate:

- Unless you have a ton of cash, you may be priced out of many foreclosure and tax auctions where you have to come up with the full purchase price within days or hours of successfully bidding at the sale.
- It will probably take you longer to accumulate wealth, because you will likely have to tie up all of your investment capital on just one or two homes at a time.
- When you start with your own money, it gives you the chance to establish a track record of successful investing in real estate, thus giving you a better chance of securing investors if and when you decide to approach them in the future.
- You're much more likely to be cautious and thoroughly research every potential acquisition before making a purchase when your own money is on the line.
- Some people can get too cautious when investing their own capital. It doesn't do you any good to invest all of that time and energy in research if you can't pull the trigger when a good deal comes around.
- All of the wealth you make—or lose—on your investments will hit your bottom line.
- If you work on just one or two properties at a time, you can be much more involved in any improvements and renovations done to the property. Your focus won't be spread too thin over many homes.
- It's much easier to keep your current job and start investing on a part-time basis when you don't have to worry about going out and finding investors and money. You can go at your own pace, develop your comfort level, and move on a property only when you're good and ready to make a move.

- When you use your own cash to buy properties, you won't be paying interest on the money, which gives you more time to get a home ready for rental or sale without the interest clock ticking your profits away.
- Investors, who rightfully want some assurances that you know what you're doing, will often help you set up requirements and controls that force you to make better investments and keep better records on your transactions than you would on your own.
- If you go it alone without any practical real estate experience or advice from someone with experience, it's likely that you will learn through making mistakes, which can be quite an expensive education.

Have a plan before you get started

Before you commit any of your own money to a real estate purchase, I suggest that you take a few steps to lay some solid groundwork. First, sit down with your family and make a budget of your household income and expenses. Make sure you can afford to spend the capital you've set aside for real estate. It doesn't make much sense to spend money on an investment property when it means that you can't afford to make your car payment or put food on the table. Discuss whether or not your family members are equipped to live in a home while renovations are taking place. If so, you can live in the house you are fixing up and save hundreds or even thousands of dollars each month by not having your current mortgage or rent payment while fixing up your latest acquisition. That money will go a long way toward covering any repairs that need to be done. That way, just as I described in my story about the Mullins family, you can buy a distressed property and build your equity position by getting the house into top shape while you're living there. Then, you can sell the property, turn it into a rental, or stay there and get a loan against your equity to finance your next purchase. As you may remember from the introduction, I used a variation of this method to get started myself. I bought properties and rented out rooms to my friends until I could afford to live on my own in my own home.

Frequently overlooked sources of capital

Of course, if you know you can't possibly live in a construction zone and you'd rather maintain your permanent residence while you invest in fixer-uppers, there may be sources of money that you haven't considered as a way to raise investment capital. If you're really serious about doing this, you can free up money by tightening your fiscal belt a few notches. Drop your cable TV, start brown-bagging your lunch to work, stop paying for Internet access and take advantage of one of the free Internet service providers, give up smoking, put off taking a vacation for a year or two, and so forth. If you look carefully and sacrifice a little, there's no reason you can't find a significant amount of regular extra cash. You just have to decide whether or not it's worth some minor sacrificing now to achieve your financial goals in the future.

Other, more obvious places to look for money are

- Your current home—If you have equity, you can refinance or get a second mortgage to pull out money. If you have good credit, you may even be able to pull some cash out of your house even if you don't currently have much equity.
- Property taxes and insurance—If you have enough equity in your home, your lender may not require you to have an escrow account to pay these annual bills, which could free up as much as a few hundred dollars per month to invest. Just be careful that you don't overextend yourself to the point where you don't have any money to pay these bills when they come due.
- Brokerage accounts—Many stock brokerage firms allow investors to borrow money against their stock portfolio. Or it

may be time to capture some of that profit you made in the last bull market by selling off some stock for cash.

- Life insurance—Check with your agent to see if you can borrow money against your policy.
- Income taxes—When you begin investing, you will be running a business out of your home, which means that you might qualify for additional tax deductions than what you're currently paying. Talk to your accountant or financial adviser about how to set up your home office and how its deductions will impact your tax burden. Adjust your tax deduction per paycheck or quarterly estimated tax payments accordingly.
- IRA or retirement account—You can often borrow money against your account. Some may even allow you to invest the actual money in the account in real estate, with the profits remaining in the account. Check with your accountant to see how much access you have to this capital.
- Gifts—Some people are lucky enough to have relatives who are willing to provide them with seed money to get a business rolling. Ask Mom and Dad or your rich old Aunt Wilma for the money you need to get started and take advantage of your good fortune by busting your tail to make things happen.
- Credit cards—Sure, paying 20 percent on your money isn't the most optimal situation. But, it is a way for you to get into the game if you can't find money anywhere else.

Maintaining a healthy amount of fear

If you have little or no real estate experience and the thought of putting up your own money to buy investment properties scares the daylights out of you, that's good. Do whatever is necessary to keep a healthy amount of fear and trepidation about putting your money on the line. A little fear keeps you on your toes and forces you to look at potential acquisitions from every possible angle before risking your money. Believe it or not, it can get quite easy to become lackadaisical about your research once you have several transactions under your belt. Just remember that one bad deal can totally offset several good ones—and if your first one is a bad one, it could knock you completely out of the game before you even have a chance to get started.

But I'm sure I don't have to remind you to be serious about your money and what you should do with it.

Summary

Although there are advantages to using only your own money to build wealth through real estate investments, it will generally take a longer time. But if you still can't figure how you can come up with the money you need to get started, don't despair. In the next chapter we'll discuss how you can gain access to other people's money for your investments. And spending other people's money can be a lot of fun—for both you and the investor!

CHAPTER 3

Finding, Enticing, and Working with Independent Investors

Now we get to one of my favorite things about living in America. There are people who have a lot of money who are always looking for good places to invest. In this country, it's possible to build a ton of wealth without ever putting large amounts of your own capital at risk. At the risk of oversimplifying, the key to working successfully with independent investors is to create win–win situations on each deal you do together. If you keep your investors happy, they will keep putting their money up and will probably eventually tell their friends about you.

Institutional vs. private lenders

Let's talk about the differences between banks and other lending institutions and private investors. First of all, banks usually have much more money available than do individuals, but banks are likely to have many more requirements that must be met in order to secure the capital you require. Lending institutions are more likely to check your credentials once and then set up a line of credit that allows you to go to work, with regular audits by the bank to make sure you're actually doing what you proposed. Individual investors usually want to be more involved in what you're doing. They may not agree to lend you any money on a deal until they've thoroughly reviewed the numbers on the deal themselves.

INVESTMENT OBJECTIVES OF LENDERS

The investment goals of these different types of investors can vary greatly. Most banks are looking to earn some sort of interest rate on your loan. They basically turn their money over by writing many loans and investments. They make a profit as their portfolio pays them back and by selling off the paper to other investors.

Private investors, on the other hand, are much more likely to be looking for a piece of the pie in addition to interest income. If an individual knows that you stand to make $15,000 by buying and flipping a property with his money, chances are that he won't be happy earning just 10 percent per annum on his investment. If, for example, a private investor put up $50,000 and you turned the property over in five months, at a 10 percent interest rate he would make just under $2,100 on his investment. Sure, that's a nice return on his money, but if he sees that you've made $13,000 to his $2,000, he'll rewrite the rules before he invests again. After all, he'll say, "I took all of the risk by putting up the cash." And to a certain extent, he would be right.

Building a track record to entice investors

So, as you can see, you have more decisions to make as you create your investment plan. Often, the decision will be made for you when the banks refuse to lend you money for your venture. Especially if you don't have any real estate experience, private money may be the only way for you to break in if you don't use your own money. If you already have some real estate expertise, a bank is much more likely to give your application a second look. Either way, however, I strongly suggest that you start by approaching investors to set up a deal-by-deal relationship rather than seeking a line of credit. Whoever puts up the cash for you will have a lot of money on the line; you will be more successful building trust if you present each transaction to him or her separately, especially if you plan on working on only one or two properties at a time. (After you've established a solid track record of success is the time to seek out that open line of credit.) In other words, don't bite off more than you can chew.

Finding investors

So, where do you find these people with all the money? And how do you approach them?

Tapping your sphere of influence

The best place to start is with your sphere of influence. Let your family, friends, and acquaintances know a little bit about what you're planning to do. Tell them enough about the potential upside to get them interested. Give them an idea of the kind of money you'll need. Don't be afraid to come right out and ask people if they want to hear about your investment opportunity. Remember that you're offering people a chance to make some money. If your sphere of influence doesn't have the kind of investment capital that you'll need, ask them to help you identify people who do. Be creative; offer your friends and family the chance to profit if they help you land an active investor.

As I mentioned earlier, one of my first investors was my grandmother, Julia Rowland. My mom and dad were also early providers of working capital. But, perhaps the best investor I've ever had was Tony Ferris, my parents' attorney. At first, Mr. Ferris would secure investment capital for me through his own network of friends and business associates. Over the years, we have refined the process and made our transactions more profitable for everyone involved. Now, 25 years later, not only is Mr. Ferris my attorney, but we continue to invest together in real estate. Sure, we have lost on a few deals over the years, but overall, we both have made a lot of money because of our relationship. And it all started because I tapped my sphere of influence to find investors.

EXPANDING YOUR OPTIONS

If you want to be a little more aggressive, place an ad in the paper or send out a focused mailing to groups of people with whom you have something in common. Focus on groups like alumni from your high school or college; clubs and organizations of which you're a member; owners of restaurants and businesses you frequent; and people with whom you do volunteer work.

Your goal during this initial investor prospecting stage should be just to get your prospects excited enough to agree to a meeting where they will learn more about your venture. Let me say that again. At this point you want only to sell them on the idea of allowing you to make a formal, detailed presentation. This may seem like a minor point, but it is important that you maximize your chances of landing each prospective investor. To do that, you'll need every possible sales tool at your disposal.

Presenting your plan to investors

Before you begin asking people for money, however, you have to prepare yourself. You're going to be seeking large sums of capital; if you don't appear organized with a well thought-out presentation of your plan, nobody's going to give you anything.

You will need some sort of document that explains who you are and why investors should provide you with money. It can be a business plan or executive summary, a prospectus, a file of sample deals, or a PowerPoint presentation. There are many fine books and software products on the market that can assist you in putting together a solid business plan, so I won't insult your intelligence by trying to explain how to create one in just a few paragraphs.

However, allow me to discuss a key part of your business plan and the best way to approach it. It's the question of real estate experience. You can't avoid this issue. You either have the experience or you don't, but even if you don't have any real estate experience, there are still ways to make your venture an attractive investment vehicle. First, focus on experience that you do have. Perhaps you've sold a home or two on your own without a real estate agent. Maybe you already own an investment property or two. You may have skills evaluating property as a home inspector, appraiser or contractor, or maybe you've done major renovations on your own home.

If you haven't actually bought, sold, evaluated, or repaired real estate, tell your prospects about any related experience you may possess. Have you owned or managed a business? Did you supervise important projects at your job? Do you have experience working with multiple vendors on a single project? Showcase your skills in project management, handling people, organizing projects, accounting, and money management.

Also, just because you don't have real estate experience doesn't mean you don't have access to it. Do you have any friends or family who work in real estate or related industries? Many real estate agents would be willing to help you evaluate properties in exchange for the promise that they will get your listing when you sell the home. An added benefit of this type of relationship is that your agent will also be on the lookout for more investment properties for you to purchase.

Even if you don't want to work closely with Realtors or other real estate specialists who would expect some business from you in return for providing their expertise, you can still strengthen your position with investors by paying for a professional evaluation of any property you plan on purchasing. Licensed real estate appraisers and home inspectors can unearth major problems with a property that you might otherwise never even know exists until it's too late. In fact, no matter what level of real estate experience you have, it is always a good idea, if possible, to have an appraisal and home inspection done before you purchase a property. It costs only a few hundred dollars and, if you're getting into real estate investment for the long haul, your appraisals and inspections will pay for themselves the first time they save you from buying a money pit.

Early investor relationships

Admittedly, when you're first starting out, you will most likely be at the mercy of any investor who agrees to put up his or her money. Unless you already have strong practical experience investing in real estate, any potential money partner will view your venture as a risky investment at best. If that's the case, your investor will probably try to dictate much of the lending and payback arrangements as well as the investor's share of any profits or losses associated with a property. In the beginning, you may just have to take your medicine until you build a track record that can put you in the driver's seat with investors. Just be careful that you don't get yourself locked into any long-term agreements that could restrict your ability to do business if your relationship should sour in the future. I suggest that you approach initial investors with the idea that you will seek out their capital on a deal-by-deal basis.

Investor relationship guidelines

When you do gain the experience that will help you call more of the shots, here are some guidelines you should follow when bringing investors on board:

- Have a written agreement so you don't have to renegotiate your arrangement every time you seek capital from the investor.

- Be sure your relationship with your investor is nonexclusive so you are not tied to a single investor.
- Have a clear understanding of how much money the investor has available for your venture. This way, you can confidently research properties that are within your reach and avoid wasting your effort on ones that are not.
- Be sure you have quick and easy access to cash so that you can move quickly on properties. Often, how quickly you can close the deal will determine whether or not you get the property.
- Your agreement should allow access to capital for repairs and renovations on homes you purchase.
- If you share each deal's profits with your investor, try to negotiate for no interest due on the money used for purchasing the property.
- An investor should have an understanding of the local real estate market (even if you have to provide the education). He or she should understand how long it normally takes to sell a property once it is put on the market and that sellers often have to lower their asking price in order to stir the interest of buyers.
- An investor should have the ability to let you do what you do without constantly interfering or requiring an unreasonable level of handholding.
- Real estate investment is an inexact science, and your investor should know that if he or she invests in enough property, eventually there will be transactions that will just break even or even lose money. (While you're building your relationship with a new investor, it's especially important that you pass on any iffy deals. If you're not positive it's a great deal, pass on it.)
- Have an understanding with your investor that, should he lack the capital or desire to put up his own money for all of the deals you bring to the table, he will introduce you to his friends and family who are potential investors.

Seek out fresh sources of capital

The beauty of a good investor is that he or she can often put you in touch with other investors. Of course, your investor won't tell anyone about you if she doesn't have confidence in your abilities—or possibly if she has too much confidence in you. If you're working with someone who has enough money to fund all your deals, and she's earning a nice profit as a result of your work, don't be surprised if she decides to keep her investment in your venture her private little secret. The danger for you in that situation is that you're relying too much on a single source of money and there's always the possibility that this source could dry up, leaving you with no investment capital at all.

Unless you have five or ten people ready and able to fund your deals on a moment's notice, you should always be seeking out fresh investment capital and better terms for yourself, and the best source of this is often the family and friends of current investors.

Keep your investors informed

Make your current investors comfortable enough investing with you to recommend that members of their sphere of influence invest their money with you, as well. Build their confidence in your performance. The best way to accomplish this is by providing your money people with regular updates and detailed records of your investment activities.

If you're working on a deal-by-deal basis, present the potential transaction as professionally as possible. Create a file that includes

- Photos of the property—both exterior and interior, if possible.
- Expected purchase price or maximum purchase price if an actual amount is unavailable.
- Value of the property—in terms of rental income and/or resale. Include a copy of the appraisal if you have one.

- Required repairs and renovations and your estimates of the amount of time and money needed to finish the job—including real estate marketing time and commissions if you're flipping the property.
- Capital required from investor to put the deal together.
- Expected return on investment.

Once the deal has been completed, that is, the property has been renovated and sold or rented—provide your investor with an updated file that shows the results. If your estimates are way off in either direction, include a specific explanation of what happened to cause the variation. For example, "We saved $1,400 because the carpet did not need to be replaced," or, "The additional two weeks and $2,500 were spent because we had no way of knowing that the plumbing throughout the first floor had to be ripped out and replaced."

In addition to keeping your investors updated and happy, this exercise also will help you fine-tune your operation. You can see where your estimates are missing the mark and which recurring surprise expenses you should begin including in your expense estimates on every property because of their frequency. Furthermore, a stack of the files I've just described will be a great tool for helping you attract bank and individual investors in the future.

Know when to fire an investor

That leaves us with just one final aspect of working with investors to discuss: when to fire them. I know it sounds a little crazy to talk about getting rid of investors when you probably don't even have any yet, but you might as well be prepared to lower the ax when the time comes.

I suspect that you're considering real estate investment as a path to financial independence. If that is indeed the case, then it means that you are currently less than satisfied with some aspect of your current way of making a living. It could be that you don't make enough money, you have to work too hard to earn what money you do make, you dislike the work you're doing, your job doesn't allow you to spend enough time with your family, or any of a thousand other reasons. The point is that you're hoping to leave those worries behind for the more satisfying situation you believe you can build through real estate. If what I've just said strikes a chord with you, then please do yourself a favor and take a few minutes to write down a description of what you're trying to escape and what you hope to find in your new venture.

Although it may seem as if I'm going off on a tangent here, I'm really not. Whether you know it or not, being "your own boss" can often mean that you trade in a single boss at your current job for the multiple bosses who dictate what you can and can't do on your own. Obviously, the most important of these new "bosses" will be the investors whom you bring onboard. Believe me when I say that the wrong investor can be ten times more unbearable than any boss you've run into so far. The point is that you should never lose sight of the reasons why you decided to get into real estate investment in the first place. If an investor becomes so overbearing or demanding that he or she makes you long for the old days of punching the time clock, fire him or her. Yes, that is another advantage of working for yourself—you can fire "bosses" whom you don't like. Investing in real estate can and should be fun as well as profitable. If doing it makes you miserable, what's the point? And if you can trace your misery back to one specific investor, then fire him or her.

Of course, you have to be smart about it. If he or she is the only investor you have, you may want to bite the bullet for a while until you can line up someone else. And, if you're not positive that it's the investor who's causing your grief, keep going over the situation until you're positive one way or the other. Another thing to keep in mind is that some investors will be more hands-on at first until they get more comfortable with you. Don't jump the gun; give people a chance to settle into the relationship before making snap judgments and try to see things from the investor's perspective as well as your own. Remember that, just like you, your investor is in the relationship first and foremost to make a profit. If you put together profitable deals, chances are that everyone will be happy.

Summary

If you decide that you'd prefer to use other people's money to invest in real estate, remember the key to working successfully with independent investors is to create win–win situations on each deal that you do together. Investment sources that you can tap include your sphere of influence, but do not have to be limited to that group, although you may have to build a track record before you can entice investors to put up the capital. You can do this by presenting a very professional and knowledgeable image and by keeping your investors informed of your real estate activities. Last, not every investor relationship is an asset, so you must be able to recognize and fire an investor who creates an unnecessary burden.

CHAPTER 4

The Value of Hard Money

Investors who specialize in purchasing distressed properties, fixing them up, and then selling them for a profit quickly discover some unique problems when seeking bank financing for find, fix, and flip projects. Unless they have a down payment of 20 percent or more, cash to cover the cost of renovations, and additional funds in reserve to cover monthly loan payments until they complete and sell the property, traditional lenders won't touch their deals.

Fortunately, there are lenders and private individuals who fill this void by making short-term, high-interest loans to real estate investors. This type of mortgage lending is generally referred to as "hard money," but it's also known by a number of different names, including equity lending, portfolio lending, rehab loans, and private financing. Most important, for investors, the individuals lending this money understand the business of property rehab, and offer programs that meet the special needs of investors in this area of real estate. And, since individuals—instead of detailed underwriting guidelines—control most hard money, these lenders are often flexible enough to customize their programs to fit the parameters of your specific deal.

Finding hard money

You can find these private lenders in your area by looking in the newspaper classified ads under "financing." Additionally, talk to other investors, real estate professionals, attorneys, title agents, and loan officers. If you network within the real estate investment community, you'll eventually stumble across the names of hard moneylenders.

Meet and interview the individuals offering access to this money. In some cases the individuals have a loan officer handling the loan process for them. When I lend hard money, John Thornton, a loan officer in my company who works closely with investors, does this job for me. According to John, the best approach to hard money borrowing is to build a solid relationship with your lender. "Get pre-approved for a set amount of funds by going through the screening process before you have a loan application on the table," he says. "Then, whether it's $50,000, $250,000, $1 million, or more, you know exactly what types of renovation projects you can seek out. Now when your lender approves a specific deal, if the property makes sense, you can move on it quickly because you're already pre-approved for the money."

Realize that hard money doesn't come cheaply. Because the loan term is so short, lenders regularly charge buyers six or more discount points, and an interest rate of 15 percent or more. As an investor you simply have to figure the cost of your money into the rehab estimate just as if it were any other renovation expense.

Hard money the Ralph Roberts way

There are as many different nuances to individual hard money lending programs as there are individuals providing access to this kind of financing. Since the investor mortgage program I have established here in metro Detroit has many features similar to other hard money programs across the country, I will describe how mine works, followed by a breakdown of some of the areas to scrutinize when you examine hard money in your own area.

We loan hard money based on the future value of the house, as estimated in a "subject to" appraisal and detailed rehab estimate.

- The purchaser may borrow up to 70 percent of the appraised value. This means that there will be at least 30 percent profit left over when the property is sold. So, if the borrower defaults on the loan, we can foreclose and get a property that will ultimately be worth more than the money we loaned out, plus any legal fees involved in the foreclosure.
- Any funds not used for the purchase are held in an escrow account to be released as renovations are completed and inspected. This provision allows us to be sure that the money we're lending is actually being spent as agreed. Lenders like to have some control over their investment.
- Our loans are available at a 16.5 percent interest rate. The interest rate may seem high, but remember that in most deals of this nature, the underlying property is renovated and sold in less than two years. The investor merely has to figure the cost of this short-term money into his or her overall expense and profit calculations.
- The note will be for a one- to two-year term, based on a 25-year amortization schedule. This means that the monthly payments are calculated as if the mortgage was going to be paid back over 25 years. Since it actually has to be paid back in one or two years, a balloon payment of the principal balance will be due once the term is completed. It is expected that the investor will have already sold the house and paid back the loan by that time.
- Monthly payments are calculated with principal and interest. We don't allow any interest-only payments.
- We don't charge any prepayment penalties. If you sell the property one day after closing the loan, you can pay us any principal and interest that is due and retire the note without additional charges.

Let the borrower beware

As you begin to work with hard money loans, be extra careful if the lender creates custom mortgage documents. It's always a good idea to have a knowledgeable real estate attorney check out any investment loan documents before signing them, especially if they are not standard mortgage documents. Keep in mind that hard money is for investment purposes only and all transactions are strictly buyer beware. The more you know about potential pitfalls and hazards of this type of lending, the better equipped you will be to protect yourself. Following are some key terms of your loan that you should know the details of before closing the transaction.

- *Points or Discount Points* A point is one percent of the loan value. For example, on a $100,000 loan, one point is equal to $1,000. Almost all hard money loans include points charged to the borrower. Be sure you know ahead of time how many will be charged, and whether the points need to be paid in cash at the closing table or if they can be rolled into the loan balance.

- *Loan-to-value (LTV)* A house's LTV is the percentage of the property's value represented by the loan amount. For example, if a home was worth $100,000 and you borrowed $65,000, then the LTV would be 65 percent. In hard money, LTV is based on the future renovated value of the property as estimated in the "subject to" appraisal. You're not likely to get a hard money loan with an LTV higher than 70 percent, and depending on your area, you may be lucky to do much better than 50 to 60 percent. Do yourself a favor and only borrow what it takes to purchase the property and make repairs. You can always collect your profits when the property sells. Make sure you have a thorough repair list since it will likely be used to determine what amount of money you can secure from the lender. Look for a conservative appraisal to ensure the value estimated is actually there. It makes no sense to fool yourself only to discover the hard way that your property isn't worth what you borrowed.

• *Amortization* The process of calculating monthly payments to pay back a loan over a fixed number of years is called amortization. If you've ever borrowed money to buy a residence for your family, you'll likely remember the loan officer talking about mortgages with a 15- or 30-year "am." That means that it would take 15 or 30 years to pay back the loan if you made the prescribed minimum payment each month. Hopefully your investment property will be sold in a matter of months, in which case the majority of the principal balance will be paid off in a lump sum at the closing of your sale. The reason you want the loan amortized over as many years as possible is because it will bring down your monthly payments and ease your cash flow.

• *Monthly Payment* A standard monthly payment that normally covers principal and interest payments. You may encounter lenders who require an escrow account set up to cover property taxes and insurance so these items can be kept current. Some hard money loans are set up where you pay just the interest due each month and no principal or escrow. Others will allow you to cover the first few monthly payments by borrowing additional funds, which are placed into an escrow account and withdrawn as each monthly payment comes due.

• *Balloon* Because the loan is amortized over many more years than the actual term, the mortgage note will come due long before the monthly payments have paid off the principal balance. Any principal balance remaining when the note comes due is known as a balloon payment. The balloon terms are extremely important to an investor. Ask for as long a term as possible—the average hard money balloon is somewhere between 6 and 24 months. Talk with your lender about writing into the contract a process for requesting and receiving extensions on the loan if the project is not completed or the home is not sold by the balloon date. There's nothing worse for an investor than to lose a profitable house to foreclosure because the work isn't completed when the balloon comes due and the loan has no provisions for an extension.

• *Prepayment Penalties* Many hard money loans have prepayment penalties, charging the investor one to three percent if the loan is paid back in the first three to six months. Some individuals who give investors access to their money want some sort of nearly guaranteed return on the loan to cover the time and expense of putting the deal together. Prepayment penalties are one way to accomplish this.

• *Closing Costs* Don't be afraid to ask your lender to explain the nature of any fees or expenses they charge you on the loan. Expect to pay normal loan costs and title premiums, which are listed below. However, if you see big fees on your closing statement that aren't on this list, find out the reasoning behind them before you agree to pay them. Normal loan costs and title premiums include:

Loan Origination Fee
Discount Points
Appraisal Fee
Credit Report
Underwriting Fee
Recording Fees-Transfer Tax
Hazard Insurance
Property Taxes
Settlement/Closing
Title Insurance
Survey
Escrow Account

• *Cross Collateralization* Most lenders will want more than the subject property to secure their loan. Don't be surprised when they ask you to put other properties or personal possessions at risk.

Loaning your own hard money

Suppose you're good at evaluating properties and you have your own money to invest, but you can't seem to find any deals. This would make you a perfect candidate to loan out your own hard money. It's a great way to make a big return on your investment without putting your money at too much risk. Additionally, you get to help other investors by providing the capital they need to do their own deals.

The best way to get started is to approach a local mortgage broker about setting up a hard money program through his office. Since you'll be providing the funding of loans, and sharing the wealth of the profits, the mortgage professional can provide marketing to potential borrowers, a loan officer to take loan applications, review of potential borrowers' credit histories, and access to reputable professional appraisers.

Work with the mortgage broker and a local real estate attorney to set up loan procedures, terms, interest rates, points, penalties, title insurance, closing costs, and profit splits. I've included on the next page a copy of my mortgage company's Investor Financing Analysis form to give you an idea of how we review hard money loan applications.

When applications come in for review, you want the deal and the borrower to be strong in the following areas:

- *The Real Estate*—The actual property on which you're writing the loan is the most important aspect of the whole transaction. Never loan money unless you are granted a first lien position on the property so you can foreclose and take the property back, if the borrower doesn't hold up his end of the bargain. Go out and inspect the property in person and make sure you understand the repairs to be made. When reviewing the deal, ask yourself if you would be willing to purchase the subject property for the amount of money you're lending the borrower. If the answer is "*yes*," then the property is probably strong enough to do the deal.

Investor Financing Analysis

Borrower: ______________________

Property Address: ______________________

____

Purchase Price:	$______	
As-Is Value:	$______	
Rehab Estimate:	$______	
Closing Costs:	$______	
Interest Rate:	______%	
Points*:	$______	
Term:	______	
TOTAL COSTS*:	$______	
Repaired Value: (Subject to Appraisal)		$______
Loan Amount:	$______	______% LTV

Conditions: | **Cleared**

______________________ | ______

______________________ | ______

______________________ | ______

______________________ | ______

______________________ | ______

(Yes = need; No = have or n/a)

Guaranty:	☐ Yes	☐ No	Address: ______
Second Mortgage:	☐ Yes	☐ No	City: ______
Record:	☐ Yes	☐ No	
Additional Security:	☐ Yes	☐ No	
Record Claim of Interest for each:	☐ Yes	☐ No	

Number of Properties: ______

Addresses: ______

Collateral* Approved: ______ Ralph R. Roberts Date: ______

Collateral Approved: ______ Date: ______

Collateral Approved: ______ Date: ______

*Only one signature needed for Collateral sign off.

Underwriting Approved: ______ John Townsend Date: ______

Quality Control Approved: ______ Alex Rehahn Date: ______

Loan Officer: ______

- *Cross Collateralization*—What does the borrower have that he's willing to put at risk to get the loan? If he's confident the property will make him a nice profit, he shouldn't be afraid to put his own real estate and personal possessions at risk.

- *Credit*—What kind of credit risk is the borrower? Does he pay his bills on time? Are his credit scores high or low? If the property is good enough, and the collateral is strong enough, credit becomes less important because your investment will be protected by a first position lien on the property.
- *Character*—Is this person trustworthy? Will he pay back this money in the agreed-upon terms? While important, character alone should never be enough to get a loan approved.

Most people who get into private financing start by lending their own money. Once you establish a track record, however, it's possible to borrow money from other individuals and banks at 7 or 8 percent interest, and then turn around and loan that money to a real estate investor at 15 or 16 percent. That leaves you a spread of 8 percent or more as well as any points you charge on your hard money loans, not to mention the ability to write more loans than you could when just using your own money.

Summary

Hard money is short-term, high-interest financing used primarily for "find, fix, and flip" real estate investment. Because the money for this kind of lending generally comes from private individuals, it is often much more flexible and investor-friendly than traditional mortgages. Loans are made based on the future value of the property as estimated in a "subject to" appraisal and detailed rehab estimate. When using hard money to purchase and renovate property, figure the cost of the money into rehab estimates just as if it were any other repair expense.

Those with some real estate knowledge and investment capital can begin lending their own hard money rather easily with the help of a mortgage broker and a real estate attorney. Hard money can be both a lucrative and a safe investment because any capital loaned out will be protected by a first-position lien on the subject property's title.

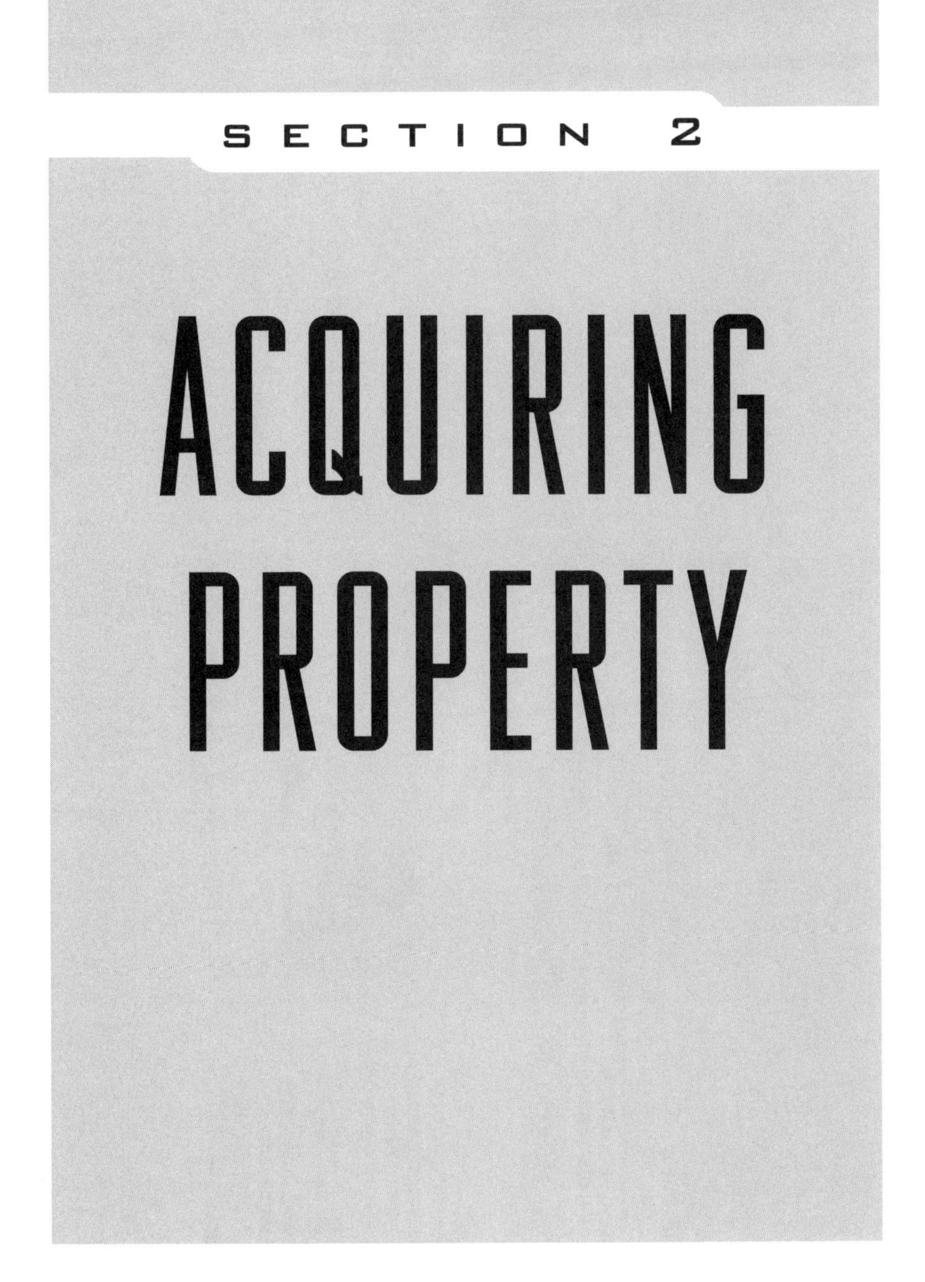

SECTION 2

ACQUIRING PROPERTY

CHAPTER 5

Understanding and Using Real Estate Appraisals

As you begin buying and selling houses, you almost certainly will be exposed to appraisals. Banks require one before lending you any money to purchase a property. Appraisals can also be useful to you as a tool to help you determine how much money you're willing to risk on a house, or whether you even purchase a property at all. Since appraisal reports can look confusing and be intimidating if you aren't familiar with them, it's important you gain an understanding of what data are included and what it all means.

Choosing an appraiser

My friend Hugo Garofalo, the president of Priority Appraisal, LLC, in metro Detroit, has been in the business for nearly a decade. "The appraiser is protecting everyone in the transaction," he says. "You want him to be someone who has no emotional attachment to the subject property. He is hired as an impartial observer to give an unbiased opinion of value."

Hugo adds that many people confuse appraisers with home inspectors. These two professionals, however, serve quite different purposes. "An appraiser determines market value based on a home's floor plan, amenities, and functionality," he says. "A home inspector seeks out structural or system problems." If you're not adept at examining a property for these kinds of defects, it's important that you hire a home inspector to look it over before you buy it. An appraisal doesn't offer any protection against defects in the house.

Since 1989, appraisers have been required by law to comply with the Uniform Standards of Professional Appraisal Practice (USPAP), a set of guidelines established by The Appraisal Foundation through its Appraisal Standards Board (ASB). The Appraisal Foundation also establishes the minimum education, experience, and examination requirements for real estate appraisers through its Appraiser Qualifications Board (AQB). Each state licenses appraisers based on standards at least as stringent as those established by the AQB. We won't go into specifics here, but if you'd like to look through the actual standards, you can visit The Appraisal Foundation's website at www.appraisalfoundation.org.

The important thing to note is that appraisers are certified by the state. This means you can check with the department of your state government that oversees appraisers to find out if someone is licensed and in good standing before counting on his or her opinion to make a huge financial commitment. Before you hire an appraiser for the first time, it's a good idea to ask the state whether he or she has any violations or suspensions on his or her record.

Approaches to estimating value

Hugo emphasizes that even when the appraiser is in good standing with the state, appraisals don't offer any guarantee that a home will sell for appraised value. "Appraisals represent the appraiser's estimate or opinion of the value of the property based on the three different approaches for determining the value," he says. These approaches are:

1. Cost Approach—A value estimate based on the cost to rebuild the house.
2. Sales Comparison Approach—An opinion of value based on a comparison of the subject property with similar nearby properties that have recently sold.
3. Income Approach—An estimate of value based on a profit the property could reasonably be expected to produce as a rental.

In terms of buying and selling residential real estate, the most accurate way to determine value by far is the sales comparison approach, according to Hugo. "If you're applying for a mortgage," he says, "and the sales comparison portion of the appraisal is weak, your loan is as good as dead." Lenders give this section of the appraisal the most scrutiny. Only if you are purchasing commercial real estate, an apartment building or other rental property, will the income approach come into play. The cost approach is looked at closely when the subject property is a one-of-a-kind building that isn't comparable to any others nearby, such as a school, church or courthouse. As an investor, you will rarely pay any more than cursory attention to that portion of the appraisal.

The parts of the appraisal report

Since all appraisers across the country use the same standard appraisal report form, the best way to teach you how to read and understand it is to go through it section by section. With Hugo's help, we'll review the data and it's importance to investors and lenders, including any red flags that may cause bank underwriters to reject the loan.

Property Description

UNIFORM RESIDENTIAL APPRAISAL REPORT

File No. sampleRR

SUBJECT

Property Address 9907 Nantuckett Cove | City Southfield | State MI | Zip Code 48034

Legal Description Lot # 8 Nantuckett Cove Subdivision | County Oakland

Assessor's Parcel No. 10-18-301-008 | Tax Year 2001 | R.E. Taxes $ 2,044.64 | Special Assessments $ N/A

Borrower Mrs. J. Borrower | Current Owner Mr. John Smith | Occupant: [X] Owner [ ] Tenant [ ] Vacant

Property rights appraised [X] Fee Simple [ ] Leasehold | Project Type [ ] PUD [ ] Condominium (HUD/VA only) | HOA$ N/A /Mo.

Neighborhood or Project Name Nantuckett Cove | Map Reference 10-18 | Census Tract 1101

Sale Price $ Refinance | Date of Sale N/A | Description and $ amount of loan charges/concessions to be paid by seller N/A

Lender/Client ABC Mortgage Company | Address 12345 American Way, Southfield Mi. 48034

Appraiser Adam Appraiser | Address 5555 Woodward , Springfield, MI 54321

NEIGHBORHOOD

				Predominant occupancy	Single family housing PRICE $(000)	AGE (yrs)	Present land use %		Land use change
Location	[ ] Urban	[X] Suburban	[ ] Rural						
Built up	[X] Over 75%	[ ] 25-75%	[ ] Under 25%				One family	80%	[X] Not likely [ ] Likely
Growth rate	[ ] Rapid	[X] Stable	[ ] Slow	[X] Owner	150 Low	New	2-4 family	0%	[ ] In process
Property values	[ ] Increasing	[X] Stable	[ ] Declining	[ ] Tenant	300 High	30	Multi-family	5%	To:
Demand/supply	[ ] Shortage	[X] In balance	[ ] Over supply	[X] Vacant (0-5%)	Predominant		Commercial	5%	
Marketing time	[ ] Under 3 mos.	[X] 3-6 mos.	[ ] Over 6 mos.	[ ] Vacant (over 5%)	165	12	(Vacant)	10%	

Note: Race and the racial composition of the neighborhood are not appraisal factors.

Neighborhood boundaries and characteristics: The subject area is bounded on the north by "A" St., east by Sax Ave, south by Jack St and the west by "C".

Factors that affect the marketability of the properties in the neighborhood (proximity to employment and amenities, employment stability, appeal to market, etc.): Subject area is comprised of primarily single family residences mixed in style and age. All forms of normal neighborhood amenities such as schools, places of worship and employment centers are within close proximity to the area. No adverse conditions noted. Commercial usage is noted along main roadways, with no adverse affect.

Market conditions in the subject neighborhood (including support for the above conclusions related to the trend of property values, demand/supply, and marketing time -- such as data on competitive properties for sale in the neighborhood, description of the prevalence of sales and financing concessions, etc.): Conventional financing is readily available at acceptable rates. Local market conditions indicate a balanced supply/demand of homes, with a typical marketing time of 3-6 months. FHA/VA, Land Contract and Cash sales are sometimes utilized as alternative forms of financing with no adverse affect on value or marketability.

PUD

Project Information for PUDs (If applicable) -- Is the developer/builder in control of the Home Owners' Association (HOA)? [ ] YES [ ] NO

Approximate total number of units in the subject project N/A . Approximate total number of units for sale in the subject project N/A

Describe common elements and recreational facilities: N/A

SITE

Dimensions 75 x 160 | Topography Level at grade

Site area 12000 Sq.Ft. | Corner Lot [ ] Yes [X] No | Size Typical for area

Specific zoning classification and description R1-Single Family Residential | Shape Rectangular

Zoning compliance [X] Legal [ ] Legal nonconforming (Grandfathered use) [ ] Illegal [ ] No zoning | Drainage Appears Adequate

Highest & best use as improved: [X] Present use [ ] Other use (explain) | View Residential

Utilities	Public	Other	Off-site Improvements	Type	Public	Private
Electricity	[X]		Street	Asphalt	[X]	[ ]
Gas	[X]		Curb/gutter	Concrete	[X]	[ ]
Water	[X]		Sidewalk	Concrete	[X]	[ ]
Sanitary sewer	[X]		Street lights	Electric	[X]	[ ]
Storm sewer	[X]		Alley	None	[ ]	[ ]

Landscaping Typical for area

Driveway Surface Concrete

Apparent easements None apparent

FEMA Special Flood Hazard Area [ ] Yes [X] No

FEMA Zone C | Map Date 6/10/95

FEMA Map No. 0001-00293D

Comments (apparent adverse easements, encroachments, special assessments, slide areas, illegal or legal nonconforming zoning, use, etc.): Site is typical for area in size and appeal with no readily apparent adverse easements or encroachments noted.

DESCRIPTION OF IMPROVEMENTS

GENERAL DESCRIPTION		EXTERIOR DESCRIPTION		FOUNDATION		BASEMENT		INSULATION	
No. of Units	One	Foundation	Concrete	Slab	No	Area Sq.Ft.	1040	Roof	Cncld [X]
No. of Stories	Two	Exterior Walls	Vinyl/Brick	Crawl Space	No	% Finished	80	Ceiling	Cncld [X]
Type (Det./Att.)	Detached	Roof Surface	Asph. Sh.	Basement	Full	Ceiling	OpenJoist	Walls	Cncld [X]
Design (Style)	Cape Cod	Gutters & Dwnspts.	Aluminum	Sump Pump	Yes	Walls	Drywall	Floor	Cncld [X]
Existing/Proposed	Existing	Window Type	Wd Dbl Hng	Dampness	None noted	Floor	Carpet	None	[ ]
Age (Yrs.)	12	Storm/Screens	Screens	Settlement	None noted	Outside Entry	No	Unknown	[ ]
Effective Age (Yrs.)	10	Manufactured House	No	Infestation	None noted			Thermopanes	

ROOMS	Foyer	Living	Dining	Kitchen	Den	Family Rm.	Rec. Rm.	Bedrooms	# Baths	Laundry	Other	Area Sq.Ft.
Basement							1					1,040
Level 1	1	1	1	1		1			1H	1		1,052
Level 2								3	2F			912

Finished area **above** grade contains: 7 Rooms; 3 Bedroom(s); 2F1H Bath(s); 1,964 Square Feet of Gross Living Area

INTERIOR	Materials/Condition	HEATING		KITCHEN EQUIP.		ATTIC		AMENITIES			CAR STORAGE:	# of cars
Floors	Carpet/Good	Type	FWA	Refrigerator	[ ]	None	[ ]	Fireplace(s) #2		[X]	None [ ]	
Walls	Drywall/Good	Fuel	Gas	Range/Oven	[X]	Stairs	[ ]	Patio	Enclosed	[X]	Garage	
Trim/Finish	Wood/Average	Condition	Avg.	Disposal	[X]	Drop Stair	[ ]	Deck	Cedar	[X]	Attached	2
Bath Floor	Carpet/Good	COOLING		Dishwasher	[X]	Scuttle	[X]	Porch		[ ]	Detached	
Bath Wainscot	Fiberglass/Avg	Central	Yes	Fan/Hood	[X]	Floor	[ ]	Fence		[ ]	Built-In	
Doors	Hollow Core	Other	None	Microwave	[ ]	Heated	[ ]	Pool		[ ]	Carport	
Avg cond/Avg quality		Condition	Avg.	Washer/Dryer	[ ]	Finished	[ ]			[ ]	Driveway	CONC

COMMENTS

Additional features (special energy efficient items, etc.): Subject has been adequately maintained and has typical features and amenities for its market area. No value given to personal property. Updates include glass block windows, new deck and Central Air.

Condition of the improvements, depreciation (physical, functional, and external), repairs needed, quality of construction remodeling/additions, etc.: Physical depreciation is based on 1% per year of effective age. No functional obsolescence was noted. Exterior inspection did not reveal any external obsolescence. Improvements are in good condition, subject has good market appeal.

Adverse environmental conditions (such as, but not limited to, hazardous wastes, toxic substances, etc.) present in the improvements, on the site, or in the immediate vicinity of the subject property: No adverse environment conditions were noted during the property inspection effecting the subject or surrounding properties.

Valuation Section

UNIFORM RESIDENTIAL APPRAISAL REPORT

File No. sampleRR

COST APPROACH

ESTIMATED SITE VALUE = $ 30,000	Comments on Cost Approach (such as, source of cost estimate, site value, square foot calculation and for HUD, VA and FmHA, the estimated remaining economic life of the property):
ESTIMATED REPRODUCTION COST-NEW OF IMPROVEMENTS:	Cost data was obtained from the Marshall and Swift
Dwelling 1,964 Sq. Ft. @ $ 68.00 = $ 133,552	Residential Cost Handbook with local multipliers utilized.
Bsmt. 1040 Sq. Ft. @ $ 12.00 = 12,480	Based on 10 years effective age, remaining economic life is
Included above =	estimated to be 50 years.
Garage/Carport 440 Sq. Ft. @ $ 15.00 = 6,600	
Total Estimated Cost New = $ 152,632	
Less Physical / Functional / External	Est. Remaining Econ. Life:
Depreciation $16,919 / 0 / 0 = $ 16,919	
Depreciated Value of Improvements = $ 135,713	
"As-is" Value of Site Improvements = $ 3,000	
INDICATED VALUE BY COST APPROACH = $ 168,700	

SALES COMPARISON ANALYSIS

ITEM	SUBJECT	COMPARABLE NO. 1		COMPARABLE NO. 2		COMPARABLE NO. 3	
Address	9907 Nantuckett Cove Southfield	9908 Nantuckett Springfield		9931 Nantuckett Springfield		938 Nantuckett Springfield	
Proximity to Subject		Same Street		Same Street		Same Street	
Sales Price	$ Refinance		$ 165,000		$ 160,000		$ 159,000
Price/Gross Liv. Area	$ 0.00 ⌀	$ 82.01 ⌀		$ 84.30 ⌀		$ 74.82 ⌀	
Data and/or Verification Sources		MLS Records Public Records		MLS Records Public Records		MLS Records Public Records	
VALUE ADJUSTMENTS	DESCRIPTION	DESCRIPTION	+(-) $ Adjustment	DESCRIPTION	+(-) $ Adjustment	DESCRIPTION	+(-) $ Adjustment
Sales or Financing Concessions		Conventional None Noted		Conventional None Noted		Conventional None Noted	
Date of Sale/Time	N/A	CL 9/00		CL 10/00		CL 11/00	
Location	Suburban/Avg	Suburban/Avg		Suburban/Avg		Suburban/Avg	
Leasehold/Fee Simple	Fee Simple	Fee Simple		Fee Simple		Fee Simple	
Site	75 x 160	70 x 160		80 x 160		75 x 160	
View	Residential	Residential		Residential		Residential	
Design and Appeal	Cape Cod/ Avg	Cape Cod/ Avg		Colonial/ Avg		Cape Cod/ Avg	
Quality of Construction	Good	Good		Good		Good	
Age	A 12 E 10.	A 15 E 10.		A 12 E 10.		A 13 E 10.	
Condition	Good	Good		Good		Good	
Above Grade Room Count (Total / Bdrms / Baths)	7 / 3 / 2F1H	7 / 3 / 2F1H		8 / 4 / 2F1H		7 / 3 / 2F1H	
Gross Living Area	1,964 Sq.Ft.	2,012 Sq.Ft.		1,898 Sq.Ft.		2,125 Sq.Ft.	-1,900
Basement & Finished Rooms Below Grade	Basement Finished	Basement Finished		Basement Unfinished	+5,000	Slab N/A	10,000 +5,000
Functional Utility	3 Bed/Avg	3 Bed/Avg		4 Bed/Avg		3 Bed/Avg	
Heating/Cooling	Gas FWA C/Air	Gas FWA C/Air		Gas FWA C/Air		Gas FWA C/Air	
Energy Efficient Items	Standard	Standard		Standard		Standard	
Garage/Carport	2 Att. Garage	2 Att. Garage		2 Att. Garage		2 Att. Garage	
Porch, Patio, Deck, Fireplace(s), etc.	Patio,Deck 2 Fireplaces	Patio Deck 2 Fireplaces		Patio,Deck 2 Fireplaces		Patio Encl Florida 2 Fireplaces	-5,000
Fence, Pool, etc.	Fence	Wood Fence		Fence		Wood Fence	
Net Adj. (total)		☒ + ☐ -	$ 0	☒ + ☐ -	$ 5,000	☒ + ☐ -	$ 8,100
Adjusted Sales Price of Comparable		0.0% 0.0%	$ 165,000	3.1% 3.1%	$ 165,000	13.8% 5.1%	$ 167,100

Comments on Sales Comparison (including the subject property's compatibility to the neighborhood, etc.): After adjustments, all comparables are considered in the final estimate of value. Effective ages assigned were based on general condition of the dwelling, taking into consideration any updating and maintenance performed or lack thereof. Emphasis placed on comparable #1 for style, square feet, and lowest gross/net adjustments.

ITEM	SUBJECT	COMPARABLE NO. 1	COMPARABLE NO. 2	COMPARABLE NO. 3
Date, Price and Data Source for prior sales within year of appraisal	No sale in past year.	No noted sales during the past 12 months	No noted sales during the past 12 months	No noted sales during the past 12 months

Analysis of any current agreement of sale, option, or listing of the subject property and analysis of any prior sales of subject and comparables within one year of the date of appraisal: The subject property is not currently listed or under contract.

INDICATED VALUE BY SALES COMPARISON APPROACH $ 165,000

INDICATED VALUE BY INCOME APPROACH (If Applicable) Estimated Market Rent $ N/A /Mo. x Gross Rent Multiplier N/A = $ 0

RECONCILIATION

This appraisal is made ☒ "as is" ☐ subject to the repairs, alterations, inspections or conditions listed below ☐ subject to completion per plans and specifications.

Conditions of Appraisal: All sales confirmed closed. All data assumed to be accurate. This is a summary appraisal report prepared in accordance with the Uniform Standards of Professional Appraisal Practice.

Final Reconciliation: Most emphasis was placed on the Sales Comparison Approach to Value. The Cost Approach was given supportive consideration. The Income (GRM) Approach was not considered as homes are normally not purchased for investment purposes.

The purpose of this appraisal is to estimate the market value of the real property that is the subject of this report, based on the above conditions and the certification, contingent and limiting conditions, and market value definition that are stated in the attached Freddie Mac Form 439/Fannie Mae Form 1004B (Revised June 1993).

I (WE) ESTIMATE THE MARKET VALUE, AS DEFINED, OF THE REAL PROPERTY THAT IS THE SUBJECT OF THIS REPORT, AS OF December 10, 2000 **(WHICH IS THE DATE OF INSPECTION AND THE EFFECTIVE DATE OF THIS REPORT) TO BE $** 165,000 .

APPRAISER:	SUPERVISORY APPRAISER (ONLY IF REQUIRED):
Signature [signature]	Signature [signature] ☐ Did ☒ Did Not Inspect Property
Name Adam Appraiser	Name Diane Reviewer
Date Report Signed December 12, 2000	Date Report Signed December 12, 2000
State Certification # State	State Certification # 1205000001 State MI
Or State License # 1205001265 State MI	Or State License # State

Section 1 (Subject)

I know this sounds basic, but it's important to make sure the Property Address and Legal Description match those of the house you had appraised. The appraisal is worthless if it doesn't cover the correct property.

Underwriters look closely at the Occupant on the fourth line. When the *Vacant* box is checked, "This makes the mortgage company really nervous," says Hugo. "They immediately think it's boarded up and completely rundown." You have to warn the lender ahead of time when the property is vacant. A check in that box without a prior explanation will severely damage your ability to get a loan.

Property Description — **UNIFORM RESIDENTIAL APPRAISAL REPORT** — File No. sampleRR

SUBJECT

Property Address 9907 Nantuckett Cove | City Southfield | State MI | Zip Code 48034
Legal Description Lot # 8 Nantuckett Cove Subdivision | County Oakland
Assessor's Parcel No. 10-18-301-008 | Tax Year 2001 | R.E. Taxes $ 2,044.64 | Special Assessments $ N/A
Borrower Mrs. J. Borrower | Current Owner Mr. John Smith | Occupant: [X] Owner [ ] Tenant [ ] Vacant
Property rights appraised [X] Fee Simple [ ] Leasehold | Project Type [ ] PUD [ ] Condominium (HUD/VA only) | HOA$ N/A /Mo.
Neighborhood or Project Name Nantuckett Cove | Map Reference 10-18 | Census Tract 1101
Sale Price $ Refinance | Date of Sale N/A | Description and $ amount of loan charges/concessions to be paid by seller N/A
Lender/Client ABC Mortgage Company | Address 12345 American Way, Southfield Mi. 48034
Appraiser Adam Appraiser | Address 5555 Woodward , Springfield, MI 54321
Location [ ] Urban [X] Suburban [ ] Rural | **Predominant** | **Single family housing** | **Present land use %** | **Land use change**

Section 1

Section 2 (Neighborhood)

The Location is extremely important to underwriters. Lenders would like to see a check in the *Urban* or *Suburban* boxes. According to Hugo, "When *Rural* is checked, it's tougher to get a loan because the property may not fit Fannie Mae lending guidelines. Mortgage companies have a problem if the property has more than five acres because they want to lend money based on the value of improvements sitting on the land, not the land itself."

If the five items immediately below Location (Built Up, Growth Rate, Property Values, Demand/Supply, and Marketing Time) aren't checked in one of the first two boxes, your loan will probably be denied. Any check in that third row of boxes usually spells trouble for the owner of the property. The condition of the neighborhood can have as big an impact on value as the condition of the house itself.

In the PREDOMINANT OCCUPANCY section, having anything other than *Owner* and *Vacant* (0–5%) checked will lead an underwriter to question the wisdom of loaning out money on this property. In residential real estate, the mortgage company wants its investment protected by making sure the house is located in a neighborhood where most people own the homes in which they live. Homeowners tend to take better care of property than tenants, which keeps values high.

Underwriters closely scrutinize the SINGLE FAMILY HOUSING portion. This provides a snapshot of the neighborhood's *Price* and *Age* ranges. In the sample appraisal, for instance, houses in the subject neighborhood range in price from $150,000 to $300,000. There are homes in this neighborhood as old as 30 years, and others that have just been built. Under *Predominant*, it says 165 and 12, which means in the subject neighborhood, the most common homes are worth about $165,000 and are 12 years old. A huge red flag will be raised if the appraisal's comparables don't reflect the neighborhood's average property as outlined in this section.

Under PRESENT LAND USE the lender wants to see mostly *One Family* for reasons stated above. If LAND USE CHANGE has anything other than *Not Likely* checked, the loan will probably be denied. "Anything that suggests uncertainty makes underwriters nervous," says Hugo.

The rest of the *Neighborhood* section isn't that important to investors or lenders unless it contains something negative. For instance, if you're buying a residential property, you want to make sure that under FACTORS THAT AFFECT THE MARKETABILITY, it says something similar to the sample appraisal rather than an adverse comment like, "Subject area is a heavy industrial zone." The PUD section refers to *Planned Unit Developments* or cluster zoning where residential, commercial, and possibly some light industrial zoning are all mixed together in a development. This part of the appraisal normally has little impact on the value of the subject property.

Appraiser Adam Appraiser Address 5555 Woodward, Springfield, MI 54321

NEIGHBORHOOD

							Predominant occupancy	Single family housing PRICE $(000)	AGE (yrs)	Present land use %		Land use change
Location	☐	Urban	[X]	Suburban	☐	Rural						
Built up	[X]	Over 75%	☐	25-75%	☐	Under 25%				One family	80%	[X] Not likely ☐ Likely
Growth rate	☐	Rapid	[X]	Stable	☐	Slow	[X] Owner	150 Low	New	2-4 family	0%	☐ In process
Property values	☐	Increasing	[X]	Stable	☐	Declining	☐ Tenant	300 High	30	Multi-family	5%	To:
Demand/supply	☐	Shortage	[X]	In balance	☐	Over supply	[X] Vacant (0-5%)	Predominant		Commercial	5%	
Marketing time	☐	Under 3 mos.	[X]	3-6 mos.	☐	Over 6 mos.	☐ Vacant (over 5%)	165	12	(Vacant)	10%	

Note: Race and the racial composition of the neighborhood are not appraisal factors.

Neighborhood boundaries and characteristics: The subject area is bounded on the north by "A" St., east by Sax Ave, south by Jack St and the west by "C".

Factors that affect the marketability of the properties in the neighborhood (proximity to employment and amenities, employment stability, appeal to market, etc.): Subject area is comprised of primarily single family residences mixed in style and age. All forms of normal neighborhood amenities such as schools, places of worship and employment centers are within close proximity to the area. No adverse conditions noted. Commercial usage is noted along main roadways, with no adverse affect.

Market conditions in the subject neighborhood (including support for the above conclusions related to the trend of property values, demand/supply, and marketing time -- such as data on competitive properties for sale in the neighborhood, description of the prevalence of sales and financing concessions, etc.): Conventional financing is readily available at acceptable rates. Local market conditions indicate a balanced supply/demand of homes, with a typical marketing time of 3-6 months. FHA/VA, Land Contract and Cash sales are sometimes utilized as alternative forms of financing with no adverse affect on value or marketability.

PUD

Project Information for PUDs (If applicable) -- Is the developer/builder in control of the Home Owners' Association (HOA)? ☐ YES ☐ NO

Approximate total number of units in the subject project N/A . Approximate total number of units for sale in the subject project N/A

Describe common elements and recreational facilities: N/A

Dimensions 75 x 160 Topography Level at grade

Section 2

Section 3 (Site)

The most important part of this section covers zoning. Make sure the property you're buying is zoned for its intended use. If the zoning is wrong, you could end up stuck with an unusable piece of real estate. For example, if you're buying a single-family house and next to Specific Zoning it says something other than *Single Family Residential*, look for the lender to kill the loan. Below that, where it says Zoning Compliance, if the *Legal* box is not checked, many lenders won't touch the loan. And those who do will likely charge a higher interest rate.

If the property is marked *Legal Nonconforming*, be cautious. If 50 percent or more of that structure is ever destroyed, it can only be rebuilt to match the existing zoning. For instance, if you bought a single-family home located in a commercial zone and the house burned down, you would not be allowed to rebuild another single-family house there. Even though the property had been grandfathered since it was built before the zoning changed from residential to commercial, now that the house is gone, any future improvements to the site must comply with existing zoning. Your permission for nonconforming use, in essence, burned up in the fire along with the structure. Be certain you're prepared to handle a situation like this before you ever buy a nonconforming piece of real estate.

Not having a check in the *Present* use box next to HIGHEST & BEST USE AS IMPROVED would really hamper your ability to get financed. This is because the current use of a property is always considered to be its highest and best use unless imminent changes in demand, zoning, the law, or some other outside force make it obvious the property will be better utilized differently.

When any utilities aren't checked in the *Public* box, if at all possible, have them tested before closing a deal, especially water and septic systems. Fixing or replacing these systems can get quite expensive really quickly.

On the far right side of this section next to the item labeled VIEW, make certain the description matches the subject property. If you are buying *Residential*, a view of *Industrial* or *Commercial* could hurt your value.

Pay close attention to the FLOOD information. Ideally, you'll want a property that is not in a flood zone. However, if the *Yes* box is checked, realize that anyone who lends you money on that property will require you to have flood insurance, which can be quite expensive. Some areas are so susceptible to flooding that flood insurance is not even available. Obviously, an uninsurable property is a good one to walk away from—and quickly!

Finally, as in the NEIGHBORHOOD section, the *Comments* are unimportant unless they contain negatives.

SITE

Dimensions 75 x 160
Site area 12000 Sq.Ft. Corner Lot [ ] Yes [X] No
Specific zoning classification and description R1-Single Family Residential
Zoning compliance [X] Legal [ ] Legal nonconforming (Grandfathered use) [ ] Illegal [ ] No zoning
Highest & best use as improved: [X] Present use [ ] Other use (explain)

Utilities	Public	Other	Off-site Improvements	Type	Public	Private
Electricity	[X]		Street	Asphalt	[X]	[ ]
Gas	[X]		Curb/gutter	Concrete	[X]	[ ]
Water	[X]		Sidewalk	Concrete	[X]	[ ]
Sanitary sewer	[X]		Street lights	Electric	[X]	[ ]
Storm sewer	[X]		Alley	None	[ ]	[ ]

Topography: Level at grade
Size: Typical for area
Shape: Rectangular
Drainage: Appears Adequate
View: Residential
Landscaping: Typical for area
Driveway Surface: Concrete
Apparent easements: None apparent
FEMA Special Flood Hazard Area [ ] Yes [X] No
FEMA Zone C Map Date 6/10/95
FEMA Map No. 0001-00293D

Comments (apparent adverse easements, encroachments, special assessments, slide areas, illegal or legal nonconforming zoning, use, etc.). Site is typical for area in size and appeal with no readily apparent adverse easements or encroachments noted.

BASEMENT | INSULATION

Section 3

Section 4 (Description of Improvement)

Since much of this section is self-explanatory, we'll simply highlight the key areas that need your close attention. Under General Description, the age of the house is listed in terms of "actual age" and "effective age." The actual age is determined by how many years have passed since the structure was first built. The effective age is determined by the appraiser after taking into consideration any improvements done to the house since it was built.

According to Hugo, "Standard appraisal guidelines say that any given house has a physical life of 60 years. That means if the structure is still standing after 60 years and no improvements have ever been made, the house will be worthless." Of course, most properties are regularly updated to some extent and each of those improvements decrease the home's effective age. You need to know how the bank looks at effective age. If a lender learns a property has an effective age of 30 or 40 years, that means the house has just 20 or 30 years of physical life left in it. Naturally, a bank would never give a 30-year mortgage on a property likely to be worthless before the loan is completely paid back. To keep from having your loan application immediately rejected, the effective age of the subject house should be 25 years or less.

Under Exterior Description, pay close attention to the item marked *Manufactured House*. If it says "Yes" there, Fannie Mae lending guidelines will not allow banks to write a mortgage on it if it was built prior to June 1976. That was when HUD instituted building code standards for the manufactured home industry. The most important fact noted in the Foundation portion will be that the house has one. If a home is not built on a slab, crawl space, or basement, Fannie Mae guidelines will never allow a conforming loan to be approved. Additionally, if a "Yes" is found next to *Dampness*, *Settlement*, or *Infestation*, your loan approval will be in serious trouble.

Notice the square footage listed for each level of the house. In the example, there is actually 3,004 square feet accounted for in the house, but only 1,964 square feet of gross living area. This is because, for appraisal purposes, basements cannot be included in square footage totals. Fannie Mae conforming loan guidelines do not recognize basements as living space, even if the basement is finished and being utilized as living space. Also realize that square footage is figured by measuring around the outside walls of the house.

The rest of this section is pretty self-explanatory, except for one note about the KITCHEN EQUIP. portion. If anything in this portion is checked, it means that the appliance is actually built-in, meaning it is a permanent fixture. It is considered a part of the house and may not be removed by an owner who sells the house without specific permission from the new owner.

DESCRIPTION OF IMPROVEMENTS

GENERAL DESCRIPTION		EXTERIOR DESCRIPTION		FOUNDATION		BASEMENT		INSULATION		
No. of Units	One	Foundation	Concrete	Slab	No	Area Sq.Ft.	1040	Roof	Cncld	[X]
No. of Stories	Two	Exterior Walls	Vinyl/Brick	Crawl Space	No	% Finished	80	Ceiling	Cncld	[X]
Type (Det./Att.)	Detached	Roof Surface	Asph. Sh.	Basement	Full	Ceiling	OpenJoist	Walls	Cncld	[X]
Design (Style)	Cape Cod	Gutters & Dwnspts.	Aluminum	Sump Pump	Yes	Walls	Drywall	Floor	Cncld	[X]
Existing/Proposed	Existing	Window Type	Wd Dbl Hng	Dampness	None noted	Floor	Carpet	None		[ ]
Age (Yrs.)	12	Storm/Screens	Screens	Settlement	None noted	Outside Entry	No	Unknown		[ ]
Effective Age (Yrs.)	10	Manufactured House	No	Infestation	None noted			Thermopanes		

ROOMS	Foyer	Living	Dining	Kitchen	Den	Family Rm.	Rec. Rm.	Bedrooms	# Baths	Laundry	Other	Area Sq.Ft.
Basement							1					1,040
Level 1	1	1	1	1		1			1H	1		1,052
Level 2								3	2F			912

Finished area **above** grade contains: 7 Rooms; 3 Bedroom(s); 2F1H Bath(s); 1,964 Square Feet of Gross Living Area

INTERIOR	Materials/Condition	HEATING		KITCHEN EQUIP.		ATTIC		AMENITIES			CAR STORAGE:	
Floors	Carpet/Good	Type	FWA	Refrigerator	[ ]	None	[ ]	Fireplace(s) #2		[X]	None [ ]	
Walls	Drywall/Good	Fuel	Gas	Range/Oven	[X]	Stairs	[ ]	Patio	Enclosed	[X]	Garage	# of cars
Trim/Finish	Wood/Average	Condition	Avg.	Disposal	[X]	Drop Stair	[ ]	Deck	Cedar	[X]	Attached	2
Bath Floor	Carpet/Good	COOLING		Dishwasher	[X]	Scuttle	[X]	Porch		[ ]	Detached	
Bath Wainscot	Fiberglass/Avg	Central	Yes	Fan/Hood	[X]	Floor	[ ]	Fence		[ ]	Built-In	
Doors	Hollow Core	Other	None	Microwave	[ ]	Heated	[ ]	Pool		[ ]	Carport	
Avg cond/Avg quality		Condition	Avg.	Washer/Dryer	[ ]	Finished	[ ]			[ ]	Driveway	CONC

Additional features (special energy efficient items, etc.): Subject has been adequately maintained and has typical features and amenities for its ... block

Section 4

SECTION 5 (COMMENTS)

The appraiser gets the chance to make note of any new or recent updates to the subject property under ADDITIONAL FEATURES. Below that, under CONDITION OF IMPROVEMENTS, are notes about how well the house has been maintained over the years, as well as the effects external forces have had on the property value. This is described in terms of three different kinds of depreciation.

- Physical Deterioration—The result of wear and tear on the house. A leaky roof or broken windows are examples of physical deterioration.
- Functional Obsolescence—The result of poor design or outmoded function, which makes the utility of the property inferior to other similar homes in the area. Examples of functional obsolescence include inadequate old-fashioned plumbing or a two-bedroom house in a neighborhood of largely three- and four-bedroom homes.
- External Obsolescence—Surrounding conditions that are a detriment to the home's salability, but out of the property owner's control. A nearby landfill or noisy airport are examples of external obsolescence.

The final part of this section, ADVERSE ENVIRONMENTAL CONDITIONS, probably won't list anything negative unless there is some toxic substance oozing out of the ground when the appraiser actually does his inspection. This doesn't mean you're off the hook for any environmental hazards. Remember, the appraiser only does a visual inspection of the subject property. If you suspect a problem in this area, get an inspection done by a qualified professional before you buy the property.

COMMENTS

Additional features (special energy efficient items, etc.): Subject has been adequately maintained and has typical features and amenities for its market area. No value given to personal property. Updates include glass block windows, new deck and Central Air.

Condition of the improvements, depreciation (physical, functional, and external), repairs needed, quality of construction remodeling/additions, etc.: Physical depreciation is based on 1% per year of effective age. No functional obsolescence was noted. Exterior inspection did not reveal any external obsolescence. Improvements are in good condition, subject has good market appeal.

Adverse environmental conditions (such as, but not limited to, hazardous wastes, toxic substances, etc.) present in the improvements, on the site, or in the immediate vicinity of the subject property: No adverse environment conditions were noted during the property inspection effecting the subject or surrounding properties.

Freddie Mac Form 70 6-93 PAGE 1 OF 2 Fannie Mae Form 1004 6-93

Section 5

SECTION 6 (COST APPROACH)

This information must be included on the appraisal report, but you can almost always ignore it if you are buying single-family residential real estate. The appraiser pulls data from a reference book, which is listed on the appraisal (in the sample appraisal it is the *Marshall and Swift Residential Cost Handbook*). This data, along with the depreciation from the previous section of the appraisal report, is used to determine the cost to replace the subject property. The property's effective age and remaining economic life are listed in this section.

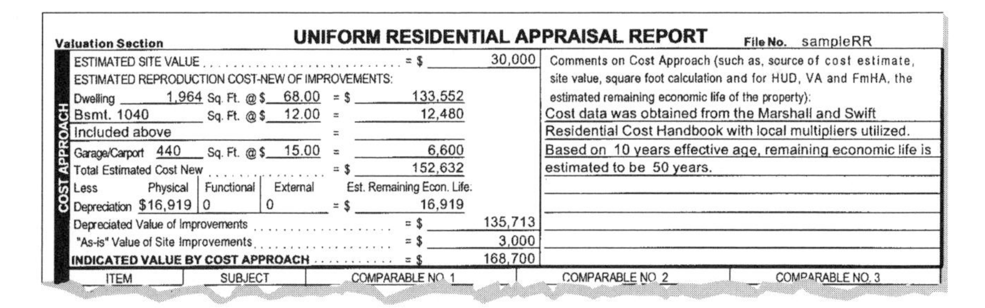

Valuation Section — **UNIFORM RESIDENTIAL APPRAISAL REPORT** — File No. sampleRR

COST APPROACH

ESTIMATED SITE VALUE .... = $ 30,000

ESTIMATED REPRODUCTION COST-NEW OF IMPROVEMENTS:

Dwelling 1,964 Sq. Ft. @ $ 68.00 = $ 133,552

Bsmt. 1040 Sq. Ft. @ $ 12.00 = 12,480

Included above =

Garage/Carport 440 Sq. Ft. @ $ 15.00 = 6,600

Total Estimated Cost New .... = $ 152,632

Less	Physical	Functional	External	
Depreciation	$16,919	0	0	= $ 16,919

Est. Remaining Econ. Life:

Depreciated Value of Improvements .... = $ 135,713

"As-is" Value of Site Improvements .... = $ 3,000

INDICATED VALUE BY COST APPROACH .... = $ 168,700

Comments on Cost Approach (such as, source of cost estimate, site value, square foot calculation and for HUD, VA and FmHA, the estimated remaining economic life of the property):
Cost data was obtained from the Marshall and Swift Residential Cost Handbook with local multipliers utilized.
Based on 10 years effective age, remaining economic life is estimated to be 50 years.

ITEM	SUBJECT	COMPARABLE NO. 1	COMPARABLE NO. 2	COMPARABLE NO. 3

Section 6

SECTION 7 (SALES COMPARISON ANALYSIS)

This section is the heart of the appraisal. This is where the appraiser stacks the subject property up against three comparables from the same neighborhood. Comparables are chosen based on their similarity to and distance from the subject property. "Ideally," says Hugo, "you want each comparable to be an exact duplicate of the subject." In reality, it's unlikely the comparables will be exactly the same, so the appraisal allows for adjustments to be made to the comparables in order to compensate for differences. It's important to note that adjustments are never made to the subject property, always to the comparables.

Fannie Mae guidelines call for fresh comparables that have sold within the last six months, which are one mile or less away from the subject. Additionally, no single adjustment line is allowed to exceed 10 percent of the sales price. For example, on a $160,000 comparable, a single adjustment line (such as FUNCTIONAL UTILITY) cannot exceed $16,000. If any of these guidelines have to be exceeded, the appraiser must explain why in the COMMENTS portion of this section.

When the appraiser makes adjustments to the comparables, they are based on the market reaction to the addition or lack of a feature, not the cost to the homeowner to install or remove that feature. For example, in Comparable No. 2 on the sample appraisal, the appraiser has determined that having a finished basement would have caused that property to sell for $5,000 more.

Take special note of these parts of the sales comparison analysis:

- Age—Both actual and effective ages are listed. If the subject does not closely match the comparables here, the bank will apply much more scrutiny to the rest of the appraisal. Beware, especially, of comparables with an actual age of more than 25 and an effective age of less than 10. Says Hugo, "An older home would have to be completely renovated and modernized to get an effective age of less than 10 years."
- Condition—"If the condition on the subject property is listed as 'fair' or 'poor,' the loan will be killed by the underwriter," Hugo says. "Banks want to see the property condition at 'average' or 'good.'"
- Bedrooms—If the subject property is a two-bedroom house, make sure that at least one of the comparables is also a two-bedroom home. "The market reacts much differently when going from a two-bedroom to a three-bedroom [home] than it does when going from a three to a four," says Hugo. There

is virtually no difference in value when comparing a three-bedroom with a four-bedroom home. However, there often is a substantial difference when comparing a two-bedroom property to a three-bedroom property.

- Gross Living Area—The closer the square footage, the better. "The banks like to see balance with the subject somewhere in the middle of the comparables," says Hugo.
- Basement & Finished Rooms Below Grade—"If the subject is on a slab or crawl space, it is unacceptable to compare it to three properties that have basements," Hugo says.

When comparing features and amenities, it's okay for the subject to have more desirable features with all the comparables adjusted upward to match it. But it's not okay for the subject to have less desirable features with all the comparables adjusted downward to match it. For example, if the subject property had 1,900 square feet and all of the comparables had 1,700, the appraisal would be acceptable. However, if all of the comparables had 2,200 square feet, the appraisal would be unacceptable because the larger houses would be artificially pulling up the value of the subject property.

To achieve accurate value estimation, the subject property must be compared to houses that need as few adjustments as possible. The more adjustments you see on the appraisal report, the more nervous you should be about the accuracy of it.

In the COMMENTS portion, the appraiser explains anything unusual about the comparables and identifies why he may have assigned more weight to one comparable over the others.

The final portion of this section lists the value the appraiser arrived at using the *Sales Comparison Approach*. Following that information are the *Income Approach* results, which will be left blank unless the subject is an income-producing property.

INDICATED VALUE BY COST APPROACH . . . . = $ 168,700

ITEM	SUBJECT	COMPARABLE NO. 1		COMPARABLE NO. 2		COMPARABLE NO. 3	
Address	9907 Nantuckett Cove Southfield	9908 Nantuckett Springfield		9931 Nantuckett Springfield		938 Nantuckett Springfield	
Proximity to Subject		Same Street		Same Street		Same Street	
Sales Price	$ Refinance		$ 165,000		$ 160,000		$ 159,000
Price/Gross Liv. Area	$ 0.00 ⊄	$ 82.01 ⊄		$ 84.30 ⊄		$ 74.82 ⊄	
Data and/or Verification Sources		MLS Records Public Records		MLS Records Public Records		MLS Records Public Records	
VALUE ADJUSTMENTS	DESCRIPTION	DESCRIPTION	+ (-) $ Adjustment	DESCRIPTION	+ (-) $ Adjustment	DESCRIPTION	+ (-) $ Adjustment
Sales or Financing Concessions		Conventional None Noted		Conventional None Noted		Conventional None Noted	
Date of Sale/Time	N/A	CL 9/00		CL 10/00		CL 11/00	
Location	Suburban/Avg	Suburban/Avg		Suburban/Avg		Suburban/Avg	
Leasehold/Fee Simple	Fee Simple	Fee Simple		Fee Simple		Fee Simple	
Site	75 x 160	70 x 160		80 x 160		75 x 160	
View	Residential	Residential		Residential		Residential	
Design and Appeal	Cape Cod/ Avg	Cape Cod/ Avg		Colonial/ Avg		Cape Cod/ Avg	
Quality of Construction	Good	Good		Good		Good	
Age	A 12 E 10.	A 15 E 10.		A 12 E 10.		A 13 E 10.	
Condition	Good	Good		Good		Good	
Above Grade Room Count (Total / Bdrms / Baths)	12 7 / 3 / 2F1H	7 / 3 / 2F1H		8 / 4 / 2F1H		7 / 3 / 2F1H	
Gross Living Area	1,964 Sq.Ft.	2,012 Sq.Ft.		1,898 Sq.Ft.		2,125 Sq.Ft.	-1,900
Basement & Finished Rooms Below Grade	Basement Finished	Basement Finished		Basement Unfinished	+5,000	Slab N/A	10,000 +5,000
Functional Utility	3 Bed/Avg	3 Bed/Avg		4 Bed/Avg		3 Bed/Avg	
Heating/Cooling	Gas FWA C/Air	Gas FWA C/Air		Gas FWA C/Air		Gas FWA C/Air	
Energy Efficient Items	Standard	Standard		Standard		Standard	
Garage/Carport	2 Att. Garage	2 Att. Garage		2 Att. Garage		2 Att. Garage	
Porch, Patio, Deck, Fireplace(s), etc.	Patio,Deck 2 Fireplaces	Patio Deck 2 Fireplaces		Patio,Deck 2 Fireplaces		Patio Encl Florida 2 Fireplaces	-5,000
Fence, Pool, etc.	Fence	Wood Fence		Fence		Wood Fence	
Net Adj. (total)		[X] + [ ] -	$ 0	[X] + [ ] -	$ 5,000	[X] + [ ] -	$ 8,100
Adjusted Sales Price of Comparable		0.0% 0.0%	$ 165,000	3.1% 3.1%	$ 165,000	13.8% 5.1%	$ 167,100

Comments on Sales Comparison (including the subject property's compatibility to the neighborhood, etc.): After adjustments, all comparables are considered in the final estimate of value. Effective ages assigned were based on general condition of the dwelling, taking into consideration any updating and maintenance performed or lack thereof. Emphasis placed on comparable #1 for style, square feet, and lowest gross/net adjustments.

ITEM	SUBJECT	COMPARABLE NO. 1	COMPARABLE NO. 2	COMPARABLE NO. 3
Date, Price and Data Source for prior sales within year of appraisal	No sale in past year.	No noted sales during the past 12 months	No noted sales during the past 12 months	No noted sales during the past 12 months

Analysis of any current agreement of sale, option, or listing of the subject property and analysis of any prior sales of subject and comparables within one year of the date of appraisal: The subject property is not currently listed or under contract.

INDICATED VALUE BY SALES COMPARISON APPROACH . . . . $ 165,000
INDICATED VALUE BY INCOME APPROACH (If Applicable) Estimated Market Rent $ N/A /Mo. x Gross Rent Multiplier N/A = $ 0
This appraisal is made [X] "as is" [ ] subject to the repairs, alterations, inspections or conditions listed below [ ] subject to completion per plans and specifications

Section 7

Section 8 (Reconciliation)

An appraisal that is not made "As is" is worthless, unless it's being used to apply for a hard money loan or other similar repair/renovation loan. If the appraisal is made subject to anything, the conditions must be met prior to the closing date or the loan will not be allowed to close.

The most important parts of the RECONCILIATION section are the date and the appraiser's value estimate. As we mentioned above, the final appraised value will almost always be the price generated by the sales comparison approach.

RECONCILIATION

INDICATED VALUE BY INCOME APPROACH (If Applicable) Estimated Market Rent $ N/A /Mo. x Gross Rent Multiplier N/A = $

This appraisal is made [X] "as is" [ ] subject to the repairs, alterations, inspections or conditions listed below [ ] subject to completion per plans and specifications.

Conditions of Appraisal: All sales confirmed closed. All data assumed to be accurate. This is a summary appraisal report prepared in accordance with the Uniform Standards of Professional Appraisal Practice.

Final Reconciliation: Most emphasis was placed on the Sales Comparison Approach to Value. The Cost Approach was given supportive consideration. The Income (GRM) Approach was not considered as homes are normally not purchased for investment purposes.

The purpose of this appraisal is to estimate the market value of the real property that is the subject of this report, based on the above conditions and the certification, contingent and limiting conditions, and market value definition that are stated in the attached Freddie Mac Form 439/Fannie Mae Form 1004B (Revised June 1993).

I (WE) ESTIMATE THE MARKET VALUE, AS DEFINED, OF THE REAL PROPERTY THAT IS THE SUBJECT OF THIS REPORT, AS OF December 10, 2000 **(WHICH IS THE DATE OF INSPECTION AND THE EFFECTIVE DATE OF THIS REPORT) TO BE $** 165,000 .

APPRAISER:		**SUPERVISORY APPRAISER (ONLY IF REQUIRED):**	
Signature		Signature	[ ] Did [X] Did Not Inspect Property
Name Adam Appraiser		Name Diane Reviewer	
Date Report Signed December 12, 2000		Date Report Signed December 12, 2000	
State Certification #	State	State Certification # 1205000001	State MI
Or State License # 1205001265	State MI	Or State License #	State

Freddie Mac Form 70 6-93 PAGE 2 OF 2 Fannie Mae Form 1004 6-93

Section 8

FLOOR PLANS, PHOTOS, AND LOCATION MAPS

Don't forget to look over the documents that follow the written appraisal report. Check the floor plan for any functional problems. Scrutinize the photos of the subject and the comparables to ensure the appraiser chose appropriate properties as comparables.

Finally, give the location map a good once-over. Ideally, the comparables should be on the same street as the subject. Since this rarely happens, make sure the subject and comparables are all at least in the same neighborhood or subdivision. As you look, keep in mind which major thoroughfares, bodies of water, railroad tracks, school district boundaries, and other landmarks serve as dividing lines between communities. It's amazing how much property values can drop if a property is located on the "wrong side of the tracks." It's not uncommon for unscrupulous appraisers to attempt to "push" the value of the subject by choosing comparables from a nearby, higher-priced neighborhood that may be on the other side of some key area dividing line.

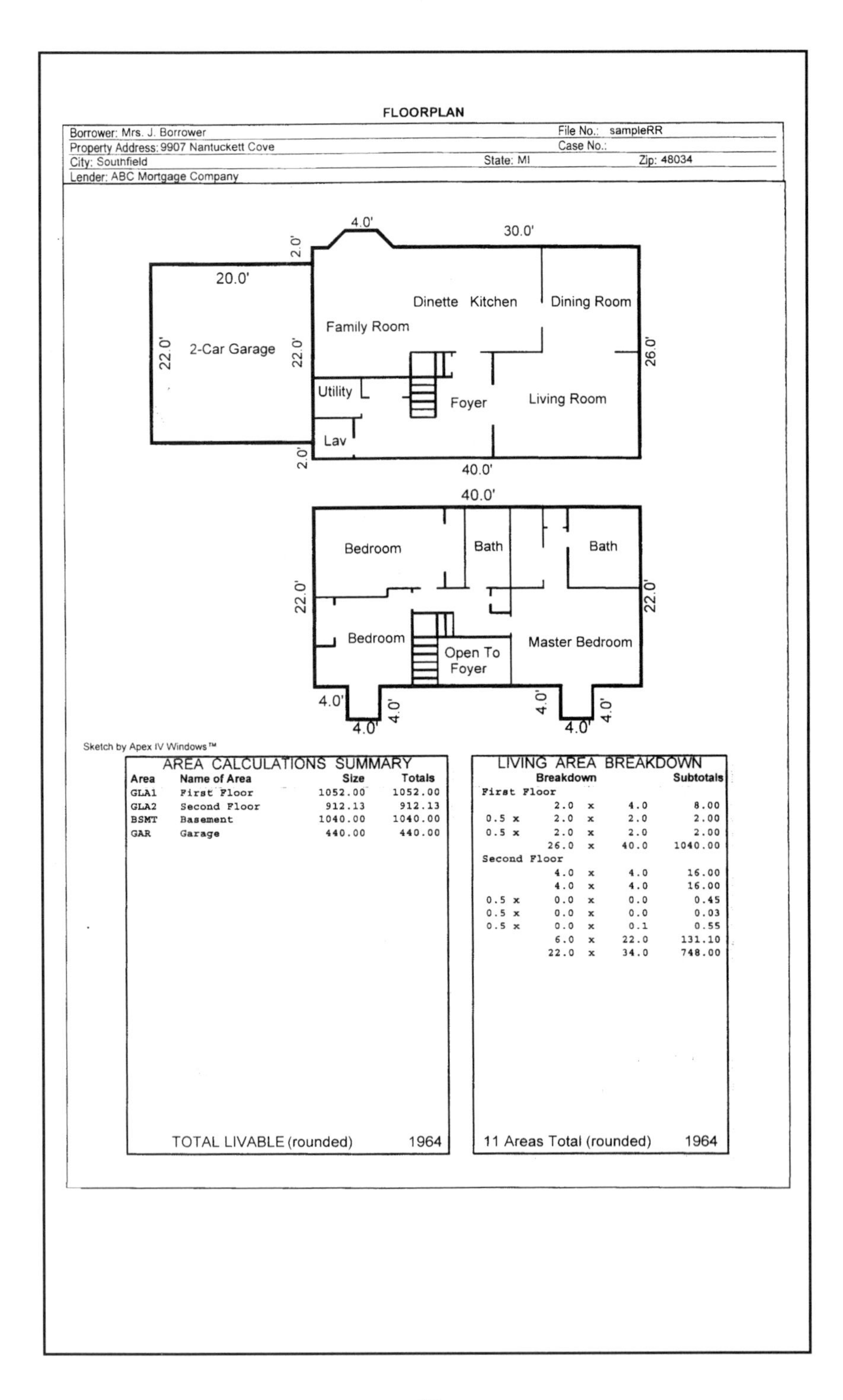

FLOORPLAN

Borrower: Mrs. J. Borrower		File No.: sampleRR
Property Address: 9907 Nantuckett Cove		Case No.:
City: Southfield	State: MI	Zip: 48034
Lender: ABC Mortgage Company		

Sketch by Apex IV Windows™

AREA CALCULATIONS SUMMARY

Area	Name of Area	Size	Totals
GLA1	First Floor	1052.00	1052.00
GLA2	Second Floor	912.13	912.13
BSMT	Basement	1040.00	1040.00
GAR	Garage	440.00	440.00
	TOTAL LIVABLE (rounded)		1964

LIVING AREA BREAKDOWN

Breakdown					Subtotals
First Floor					
	2.0	x	4.0		8.00
0.5 x	2.0	x	2.0		2.00
0.5 x	2.0	x	2.0		2.00
	26.0	x	40.0		1040.00
Second Floor					
	4.0	x	4.0		16.00
	4.0	x	4.0		16.00
0.5 x	0.0	x	0.0		0.45
0.5 x	0.0	x	0.0		0.03
0.5 x	0.0	x	0.1		0.55
	6.0	x	22.0		131.10
	22.0	x	34.0		748.00
11 Areas Total (rounded)					1964

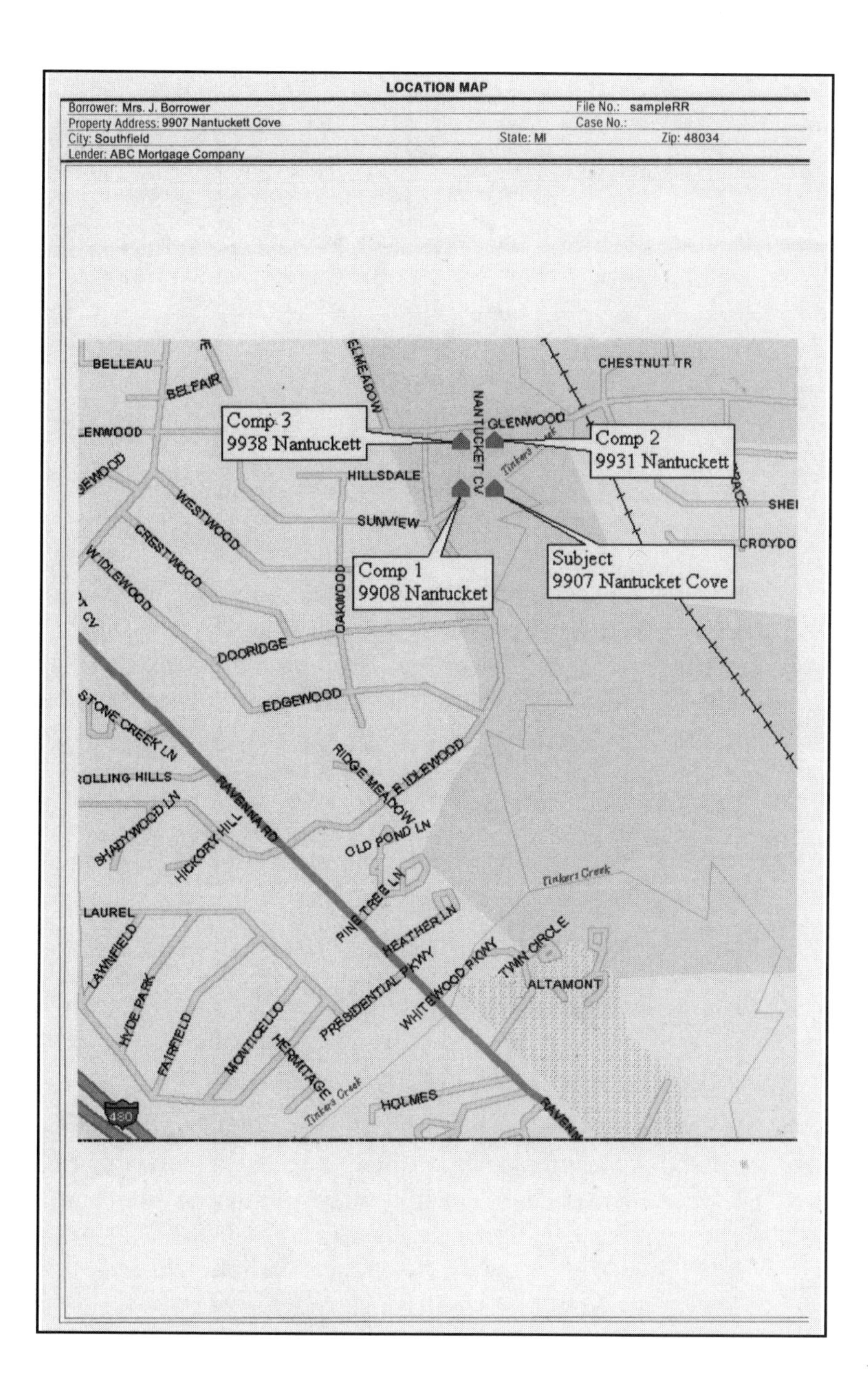

LOCATION MAP

Borrower: Mrs. J. Borrower		File No.: sampleRR	
Property Address: 9907 Nantuckett Cove		Case No.:	
City: Southfield	State: MI		Zip: 48034
Lender: ABC Mortgage Company			

Drive-by appraisals

Full appraisals at a few hundred bucks a pop may be too expensive to utilize when you're simply evaluating investment property to decide whether or not you want to purchase it. This is when a drive-by appraisal can be an effective tool. In these scaled-down appraisals, the appraiser bases his opinion of value on a combination of the outside condition of the home and property information found in city assessment records.

The value estimated by drive-by appraisal is based on several assumptions:

- Assessment records are correct—According to Hugo, some cities where he does business haven't updated their records in more than 40 years. The general rule of thumb is that smaller municipalities tend to have accurate assessment information because of frequent updates, while larger cities usually have less accurate data since regular updates are not a priority.
- The interior of the house is in marketable condition—With a little experience, you should be able to determine this on your own or you can always hire a home inspector to do it for you. In properties you cannot enter before making a decision whether or not to purchase them (such as those sold at foreclosure auctions), the exterior condition will help you make assumptions about what the inside is like. We'll cover that more thoroughly in Chapter 7 about foreclosures.
- The property is largely similar to other homes in the neighborhood—The sales comparison approach will generate inaccurate results if the subject property does not match the houses used as comparables.

A drive-by appraisal can offer an educated investor many of the benefits of a full appraisal at a fraction of the price.

Summary

Appraisals are an important tool used by real estate investors and the banks that lend them money. An appraisal is simply an estimate of a property's value. Professional appraisers are licensed by the state and must comply with the Uniform Standards of Professional Appraisal Practice. They use three different methods to arrive at an opinion of a property's value. The most important one is the sales comparison approach, which compares the subject property to three similar properties in the same neighborhood that have recently sold.

A drive-by appraisal is a scaled-down version of a full appraisal where the data used to arrive at an estimate of value is based on the exterior condition of the property and information obtained from city assessment records. This type of appraisal assumes the assessment records are correct, the interior of the house is in marketable condition, and the subject property is largely similar to other homes in the neighborhood.

CHAPTER 6

Making Money on Cash Buys and Distressed Properties

Once you've got money matters squared away, it's time to start acquiring properties. One of the best ways to get your feet wet is to seek out people who are willing to sell their property at a discount either because it is in need of repair work or because they need to divest themselves of the property quickly for some reason, or both.

Investing in distressed properties

Often, when a home gets past a certain state of disrepair, the owner has neither the inclination nor the know-how necessary to get the house back into shape. In other cases, someone inherits a property that he or she would rather sell at a discount than put the time and money into repairing.

These kinds of properties can often be found by scouring the For Sale By Owner (FSBO) ads in your local newspaper or by working with a Realtor who has access to the Multiple Listing Service (MLS). The MLS is the database of properties for sale that are being represented by Realtors. Only members of the real estate board have access to this list. The general public cannot view it without a Realtor. Check listings for phrases like, "Sold as is," "Handyman's Special," "In need of a little TLC," and "Needs a little work." These are normally signs that the home is distressed. Sit down with a real estate agent and lay out your plans for property acquisition. Whether you're hoping to buy two properties per year or 20, a smart Realtor will recognize the benefits of taking good care of you. With the average buyer remaining in each home for about five years at a time, a good salesperson will gladly pamper any prospect who plans on purchasing multiple houses in that same time frame.

If you sense that a real estate agent will be especially good at locating cash acquisitions, make it worth his while to bring you deals. If you plan on flipping properties, offer your Realtor the opportunity to represent you as the buyer and again when you list the property following renovations. If he knows that he can earn a minimum of two commissions on each house he finds for you, he will likely put some solid time and effort into locating properties for you. Also, talk to the agent's broker or your real estate attorney to find out if it's legal for you to pay the salesperson a finder's fee for helping you locate and purchase rental properties.

Cash acquisitions

There are plenty of reasons why a homeowner might want or need to sell quickly. They can be job related, such as a transfer to another city, or financial, such as losing an income, making the home unaffordable; the threat of foreclosure; or paying the price for some personal excess such as alcoholism, gambling, or drugs. Sometimes the courts order that a property be sold as quickly as possible as part of a divorce or probate proceeding.

Again, FSBO ads and the MLS are a good source for these kinds of sellers. Keep an eye out for recently listed properties that are priced to sell—meaning they are listed at the same price as or slightly lower than similar homes in the neighborhood. When you find one of these, you have nothing to lose by making a cash offer below their asking price. Let them know that you can close almost immediately. If indeed the homeowner is motivated to sell quickly, he or she might accept a lower cash offer from you over a higher offer from a buyer who needs financing or can't close quickly.

How to Locate Cash Acquisitions

If you want to be aggressive in seeking out potential cash acquisitions, buy an ad in the real estate or classified sections of your local paper or in a direct mail coupon package (like Val Pak Coupons) sent out in your area. Want to be even more aggressive? Start networking or a direct mail campaign focusing on probate, foreclosure, divorce, and bankruptcy attorneys. Let them know that you are ready, willing, and able to make cash offers on any properties they need to divest. Contact the courts that handle probate, divorce, and bankruptcy and find out how they handle sales ordered by the court.

You can also go directly to homeowners who are facing bankruptcy, divorce, and foreclosure. We'll discuss using direct mail to contact people in foreclosure in the next chapter, but you could apply the same concept to other groups—such as those in bankruptcy or divorce—who would be in a position to consider selling their home to a cash buyer. I know that this may sound a bit distasteful, as if you're preying on people who are having problems, but it's not if you approach it properly. In fact, you may be providing a valuable service by making available the cash they need. In some cases, you can be the difference between their getting some money in their pockets from the sale of their home or simply losing the home outright with nothing to show for it. And, if you've ever faced the same situation they're going through, you could be a great source of information and advice as well as reassurance that others who have been in their shoes have survived to tell about it.

Put your advertisements and flyers anywhere that you might find people who are in need of money. Post them at the courthouse, on the bulletin board in the laundromat, and near shuttle-bus stops, the pawnshop, the bail bondsman, and the auto title loan companies. Use you imagination and I'm sure you'll think of more.

The Advantage of Cash Acquisitions

One of the reasons why these types of cash acquisitions are so good when you're just starting out in real estate investment is because they allow you an opportunity to thoroughly evaluate a home before purchasing it. You will be buying directly from the homeowner rather than through a forced sale brokered by some third party—such as a foreclosure or tax auction. We'll get into more detail about these types of acquisitions in future chapters, but in many instances you will not have a chance to closely examine the inside of a property before buying it at a foreclosure or tax sale.

Conduct a Thorough Evaluation

The key to your success will be your ability to evaluate properties. If you don't have any real estate experience, be cautious when you first start out. When you visit potential sellers, don't be afraid to bring along a Realtor, builder, home inspector, appraiser, or some other person with a better grasp of home values. If you have to go by yourself, take a camera and shoot plenty of photos so that someone can help you evaluate the property after the fact. Take your time and jot down lots of notes.

Walk slowly around the outside of the house. Look for cracks in the brick or evidence of warping or weather damage to siding. Examine the roof. If it has shingles on it, how many layers are there? Are the ends starting to curl or can you see "lines" going down the roof because the shingles have begun to shrink? If the property needs a new roof, you'll most likely be looking at an investment of a few thousand dollars or more if you have to hire someone to do the work for you. Take photos so you can get a roofer's opinion of what work needs to be done, if any. Check out any wood trim for signs of dry rot or termites. Look at the windows. Are the casings wood, aluminum, or vinyl? Are there gaps between the casing and the house? If they're double-pane windows, is there fog or moisture between the inside and outside glass? Windows are another area that can mount a steep bill rather quickly. Take notice of any cracks in the pavement and the condition of the yard, landscaping, and any porches, decks, and fences. Make notes of anything outside the home that strikes you as strange, ugly, or somehow out of place there. If there is any debris in the yard—such as automobiles, scrap metal, old furniture, or anything else that seems especially heavy or hard to remove—make sure you find out from the owner whether or not they plan to leave it behind. Figure into your repair and renovation estimates any cost associated with debris removal. Little things like that, which may seem insignificant before you actually have to pay for them, can have a huge impact on your bottom line.

Inside the house, spend a little extra time in the kitchen and bathrooms. Problems with these rooms can quickly eat up any profit you might have in the house. Plus, they are two of the most important rooms when it comes time to sell the home. Don't be afraid to turn on the faucets to check for leaks and the level of water pressure. Examine the cupboards and drawers to make sure they are sturdy and open and close properly. Make note of the condition of paint, wallpaper, and carpet throughout the home. If you plan on flipping the home, you'll likely have to remove all wallpaper and bright or pastel paints and carpets. The property will sell more quickly if the colors are neutral—various shades of gray and beige. Look closely at the walls and ceiling for signs of water damage. Turn on light switches, appliances, and heating and cooling units to make sure things are working properly.

INTERVIEW THE SELLERS

In addition to touring the home, you can learn a lot about its condition by talking to the owners. Ask questions and listen carefully to what they have to say. Many homeowners will offer up all kinds of unsolicited information if you let them ramble without interruption. Here are some of the questions that might be useful:

- How long have you lived here?
- Do you have any kids? Do they live with you?
- Any pets? What kinds? Did they have the run of the house?
- Is there any reason why you're looking to sell this home quickly?
- When were you hoping to be out of the house?
- How quickly do you want to close on this sale?
- Is there any appliance or fixture you'd want to take with you when you move?
- How old are the roof, furnace, central air conditioning unit, hot water tank, etc.?
- Have the electrical or plumbing systems ever been replaced? Do you know how old they are?
- Have you ever experienced any problems with your sewer or septic?
- Has the home ever been severely damaged by any natural disaster like a fire, earthquake, tornado, hurricane, or flood?
- Are there any deadlines that are out of your control that dictate the date by which you must have the home sold?
- Do you have more than one lien on the property? How much do you owe on each lien? What financial institution, company, or individual holds the mortgages?
- Are there any IRS or state tax liens on you or your property?

- Do you owe back property taxes? Are there any special assessments or fixture filings owed on the house?
- How much were you hoping to get for the house?
- How much do you think the house is worth?
- Have you talked to anyone else who buys properties for cash about this house? Have they made any offers to you yet? How much is the highest offer you've received for your home?

When interviewing sellers and inspecting properties, use a little common sense. If the people have lived there for 20 years, the inside is immaculate, the yard is well manicured, and everything is sparkling clean, it's a safe bet that they've taken pretty good care of the home. On the other hand, if the grass hasn't been cut in two months, every spare corner of the home is piled with dirty clothes and garbage, half the kitchen cabinets are missing doors, and there's more fungus than porcelain visible in the bathroom, chances are that the owners have taken equally bad care of the home's vital systems.

The Federal Home Loan Mortgage Corporation (FHLMC), also known as Freddie Mac, has an excellent publication called "A Consumer Home Inspection Kit" that really gets into the nitty-gritty of looking over a home. You can get a copy online at their website (www.freddiemac.com) or by calling Freddie Mac at 1-800-FREDDIE (373-3343).

Valuing a property

Assemble a team of experts to help you figure out the expenses involved in getting the property in shape. After you've thoroughly examined the property, consulted with your advisers, and figured out what you'll have to spend on the property, decide how much the property will be worth when you're finished with it. You can accomplish this by getting a licensed appraiser or Realtor involved.

Appraisers and real estate agents have access to tools that allow them to easily research comparable sales in a neighborhood. By looking at what similar homes in the same area sold for, you can come up with a reasonable estimate of your property's value.

Determining your offer

If you're planning on flipping the house for a quick profit, use this value as a starting point. Work backwards by subtracting all of your expenses from the number—don't forget to include real estate commissions, interest on borrowed funds, back taxes, recording fees, and closing costs. Then figure out how much of a spread you need between how much money you put into the house and what you expect to pull out of it when you sell. The smaller the spread you're willing to accept, the better chance you have of outbidding other investors for the property. But don't allow the spread to get too thin, or the deal could easily bite you in the butt. That's because any expenses you don't anticipate and any sales price that comes in below your estimated value of the property will come directly out of the spread, meaning your profit will be slashed. Believe me, there are few things more disappointing than putting a ton of time and money into a property only to discover at the end of the project that you only broke even—or even worse, that you lost money on the deal.

If you're buying the home as a rental, you can afford a slimmer spread. Your real determining factor will be the amount of positive cash flow the property can provide. Figure out what your monthly payment on the property will be—in addition to principal and interest, don't forget to include taxes, insurance, maintenance, and any utilities you plan to carry for the tenant. It's a good rule of thumb to earmark 20 percent of the projected monthly rent payment for unexpected miscellaneous expenses. You may go months and months without any problems, but when something major—like a furnace—needs major repairs or replacement, you'll be glad that you were setting the money aside.

Subtract that expense number from the monthly rent you expect to receive on the property. How much cash flow is worth the time and effort of being a landlord is something you'll have to determine on your own. Simply breaking even or even losing a little cash flow each month might be worth it if the property is in an area where property values are on the rise.

PRESENTING YOUR OFFER

Once you've figured out what you're willing to pay for the house, it's time to make a written offer on it. I recommend that you hire an attorney to at least put together a basic fill-in-the-blanks agreement. This will save you a lot of time and money over the long run. Ask your lawyer to include language that makes your offer contingent upon an appraisal of the property. If the homeowner accepts your offer, get everything signed so you don't lose the sale. Then—and I can't emphasize this enough—hire a licensed appraiser and/or a certified home inspector to look at the property so you know exactly what you're getting into, especially if you have limited or no experience buying real estate. There are so many things that can go wrong with a home, it's in your best interests to take advantage of the years of experience appraisers and home inspectors have in evaluating property.

Tending to the legal details

As for the mechanics of the actual transaction, real estate laws vary so greatly from state to state that it would be impossible to present them here. I suggest that you find a good attorney who specializes in real estate law and pick his or her brain about the laws and regulations in your area before you start buying and selling property. Resist the urge to simply talk to your family or corporate lawyer. In most areas real estate law is in a state of constant change, so you should consult with someone who spends all of his or her time immersed in that specialty of the legal profession.

The chain of title

Although I'm not discussing the mechanics of your transactions, I do want to make an important point about one key aspect of your purchases. Don't ever buy a house without title insurance or, at a minimum, a complete title search. You have to make sure the person who is selling you the property has a legal right to actually make that deal with you. Depending on the state in which you live (there are one or two states that don't have title insurance), there are title companies and attorneys you can hire to do title searches for you. If they discover that the title to the property is free of clouds—potential ownership claims by other individuals—they will sell you an insurance policy that says they will protect you from any person who comes forward claiming an interest in the property following your purchase.

Because title information is a matter of public record, you can also conduct title searches on your own. To do this, visit your county's Register of Deeds office and ask the staff to explain the procedures in place for individuals who wish to perform title searches. Of course, keep in mind that if you search the title on your own, there will be nobody there to insure the title if you miss something and someone shows up in the future making an ownership claim on the property. Also, if you flip the house after renovations, the odds are good that your buyer will want title insurance on the purchase. So any defects in the chain of title will show up there and you'll have to pay the price of correcting them.

Insuring a Clear Title

At the risk of belaboring this point, let me drive home the importance of title insurance by telling you a short personal story about one of my first transactions.

Early on in my real estate career, I met a woman in metro Detroit who was looking to sell her home for cash. She told me that her daughter was a co-owner of the home and she would have no problem getting the daughter to sign off on the deal. I made an offer that the mother accepted and quickly closed the transaction on my own. I then moved my things into the house. The thought of purchasing title insurance crossed my mind, but because I didn't have a lot of money at the time (and because I was a little overconfident), I decided I could get by without wasting a few dollars on that.

After living in the house for about six months, I took a trip with some friends to Indiana for the Indianapolis 500. When I returned to the house, I discovered that my key didn't work anymore. Someone else had moved in while I was gone.

I eventually discovered that another daughter of the woman who sold the property to me had moved into the house with her family—a husband, several children, and a large Doberman! It turned out that this woman was actually the co-owner of the property with her mother, not the sister who had signed off on the deal. I had the right mother but the wrong daughter! The daughter who participated in the sale possessed no legal claim to the property she was selling. This other daughter—who actually was the legal co-owner with her mother—had never agreed to sell. And now she had moved back into the home claiming that because she had never agreed to sell it, she still owned it. I had decided not to pay a few dollars for title insurance, and now I was in the middle of a legal nightmare.

When I told my attorney what had happened, after he finished berating me for not getting title insurance, he told me that I had two options in fighting their claim to the house. I could move in with them and stay there until they gave up and left, or I could leave them there and fight in court. I strongly considered the first course of action, but finally settled on the legal battle. Needless to say, I now pay close attention to the chain of title on a property before I buy it.

After eight years in court I ultimately got most of my money back, but the lesson of this story is that you can save yourself a lot of money and grief by purchasing title insurance on every property you acquire. And, it's a good idea to hire an attorney, title company, or closing coordinator to close your transactions. Especially if you're just getting started in real estate, these people and organizations will help you close your deals properly and make sure the transfer is handled in a smooth, professional manner.

Whenever you're tempted to sidestep title insurance, just think of my story. Because I thought I knew it all, I did not use an attorney, I did not use a title company, and I put all of the closing papers together and closed the transaction myself. Because of my ego and misguided desire to save a few bucks, I created a problem that almost short-circuited my real estate career before it even got going. Fortunately, I was able to survive this incident and look back on it as a learning experience. But a misstep like this could easily wreck a budding real estate investing career, so take the necessary steps to ensure that it doesn't happen to you.

Summary

Once you've got money matters squared away, it's time to start acquiring properties. One of the best ways to get started in real estate investing is by finding motivated sellers who either want or need to sell quickly. Be sure to do a thorough inspection of the property before you determine your offer, and always check the chain of title and get title insurance. Before you begin, seek out the advice of a good real estate attorney to help you understand the laws of your state. Knowing what to expect ahead of time can save you time and money once you're ready to invest.

CHAPTER 7

Investing in Bank Foreclosures

I've been working foreclosures almost since the beginning of my real estate career. Unfortunately, I learned about them from first-hand experience. Although I was doing well financially at the time—with a relatively high net worth—my assets were extremely illiquid. Being a cocky kid, I had literally set myself up for failure by structuring the mortgage on a newly purchased property so there were large principal balloon payments due every quarter. I was planning to pay that loan off in record time and own the home free and clear, but I had leveraged myself so much that my ability to make those balloon payments was entirely too dependent on my future earnings. I'd left myself no margin for error to cover my payments if I had a less than stellar month selling real estate.

To make matters worse, when the foreclosure started, I didn't even tell anyone about it. I was too embarrassed to ask for help, even though there were many people around who could have helped me. I finally explained the situation to my parents about three hours before I had to leave the house for good. And the only reason I told them was because I needed to borrow their truck to move my possessions out of the house. Obviously, by that time it was too late for them to help me and I lost the house and the equity I had built up in it.

Offering solutions to homeowners facing foreclosure

Looking back on it now, I'm glad to have gone through that experience—even though I wouldn't wish that kind of misfortune on my worst enemy. Because of my foreclosure, I became interested in that area of real estate and I learned a great deal about the psychology of people going through foreclosure. Often, they are embarrassed, confused, desperate, and in denial. Every phone call they receive (assuming that their phone hasn't been turned off) seems to be from someone demanding money from them. They usually have little knowledge of the foreclosure process, and many people use misinformation in an attempt to manipulate them. There are very few people they trust because they have had to deal with so many people who seem to have an ulterior motive.

I began to investigate and learn about the foreclosure process and how, as a real estate professional, I could help people facing it. I began developing programs that helped me find and help people facing foreclosure. Believe it or not, I quickly found that in most cases, the best possible thing people facing foreclosure could do was to sell their home. This way, they might be able to keep some of the equity they had built up, instead of losing the property with nothing to show for years of making mortgage payments. Additionally, selling the property allowed them to protect their credit rating by keeping an actual foreclosure off it. The large majority of my foreclosure business came in the form of either listing and selling their homes or purchasing them for cash and reselling them at a profit.

So the good news for you as an investor is that you can provide a service to homeowners—in this case buying their homes for cash—that will allow a family to keep a foreclosure off their credit rating and maybe even help them to keep any equity they had built up. You will be helping to put the foreclosure behind them. Even if you're not convinced that you're offering valuable assistance by purchasing a foreclosure property directly from the homeowner, just realize that if you don't buy it, another investor or the bank holding the mortgage will most likely end up owning it. If someone other than the homeowner is going to profit on the house, why shouldn't it be you?

How you can profit from foreclosures

Even if you simply don't have the personality necessary to talk to people in foreclosure, you can still make money investing in these kinds of homes. The beauty of this area of real estate from an investor's perspective is that you often have three opportunities to purchase each property that eventually gets sold:

1. Buy the property from the homeowner before the foreclosure auction.
2. Acquire the home by being the highest bidder at the foreclosure auction.
3. Purchase the house from the foreclosing bank after the foreclosure auction.

You could easily make large profits by focusing on just one of these areas. But, because the research and contacts you develop from one area will almost always help you achieve success in the other two areas, it makes sense to go after all three types of purchases on each property you track. I'll spend some time on each of these areas, but first it's important that you understand the foreclosure process and the role each involved party—from the bank to the borrower to the investor—plays while the affair runs its course.

Why people lose their homes

Today more people are facing foreclosure than at any time since the Great Depression, and the number of families in trouble grows steadily. The foreclosure rate has reached epidemic proportions, with between 4 and 5 percent of all the homes in America currently either in foreclosure or threatened by foreclosure because the homeowners are 30 days or more behind in their mortgage payments.

There are many reasons why people end up in this situation, but the major causes usually have to do with a loss of income or mismanagement of funds by the homeowner. People find themselves at risk of losing their homes because of unemployment, illness, the death of a breadwinner, gambling and drug addiction, legal and tax problems, personal and emotional issues, divorce, and any of a hundred other reasons.

Keep in mind that people currently in foreclosure didn't arrive there overnight. A bank can't just seize a home from the homeowners because they're a few days, or even a month or two, late on their house payment. In fact, most financial institutions don't even begin the foreclosure process until a mortgagor is three or more months behind on the payments. Now, more than ever, many banks try to work things out with their customers before foreclosing on their homes. Financial institutions—especially the largest ones—don't usually want to acquire real estate in this manner. They would much rather have a customer paying his or her mortgage on time than own a single-family residence. They look at a performing mortgage note as a money-making asset, while viewing a bank-owned property as an expense that will cost them money until they convert it into cash (something to keep in mind when dealing directly with banks' real estate owned, or REO, departments).

Understanding the foreclosure process

Here's a quick outline of the foreclosure process, but keep in mind that every state has different laws, regulations, and procedures.

This description should just be your jumping off point. It's up to you to learn the unique process of your individual area.

- The homeowner stops making his mortgage payments.

- After 15 to 30 days the bank sends a notice reminding the homeowner that payment is due and interest and penalties will accrue if payment is not made.

- The bank continues to send letters and turns the account over to its "collections" or "loss mitigation" department, which begins making phone calls and threatening foreclosure if the borrower does not bring the account current.

- When the delinquency approaches 90 days or more, the bank will send more forceful correspondence—usually drafted and signed by an attorney—explaining that foreclosure is imminent. For some banks, this stage is the last opportunity for the homeowner to either bring current what's owed on the mortgage or negotiate a forbearance agreement with the bank that adjusts the loan so the borrower can get back on track.

- When the bank actually begins the foreclosure process, in most states, the bank is required by law to post a public notice of its intent to exercise its right to auction off the home for what's owed on the note. This public notice usually takes the form of a classified advertisement in the county's prominent daily newspaper or weekly legal newspaper. Usually this notice will be posted on multiple dates in the same location before the sale actually takes place.

This notice contains information that may include such items as the names of the mortgagor (borrower) and mortgagee (lending institution); information about the mortgage note such as the amount of money owed and the interest rate; the date, time, and location of the foreclosure auction where the property will be sold; terms of the sale; the property's legal description and/or address; the name and location of the attorney or substitute trustee conducting the foreclosure auction; the amount of time in the property's redemption period, if applicable; and any other data that may be pertinent to a particular location's laws and customs.

• The property is auctioned to the highest bidder at the appointed time and place if the homeowner does not pay off the note, work out a new payment arrangement with the bank, or use some other method (such as bankruptcy) to stop the foreclosure sale. These sales might be conducted on behalf of the bank by the County Sheriff's Department or by an attorney or substitute trustee—different methods are more common in various states around the country.

The bank that holds the foreclosed-upon lien normally leads off the bidding with the amount of principal, interest, fees, and foreclosure expenses owed on the property. If no investor offers a higher bid, the property is turned over to the bank's REO department to be prepared for sale. In most areas, this sale wipes away any liens—other than back property taxes and, in some cases, on the property's title that are junior to the mortgage sold at the auction. A fixture filing is when the homeowner borrows money to add a fixture to the property, such as a hot water tank, driveway, or new furnace, and the lender places a lien on the property with that item as collateral. Because that item is an integral part of the structure, in some states, a fixture filing is not wiped away by a foreclosure even if it is a junior lien.

• At some point following the foreclosure auction the new owner of the property—whether it be the bank or an investor—takes possession of the house. In some states, such as Tennessee, the purchaser has the right to immediately take possession. In other states, such as Michigan, there is a statutory redemption period during which the former homeowner retains the right to possess the property (for up to 12 months in Michigan) and redeem the house by paying the buyer back his or her purchase price plus interest.

• Once the bank or investor gains the right of possession, he or she may have to use the court system to seek an eviction if the former homeowner refuses to move out. In most places this will take anywhere from 30 to 90 days to complete. In the end, if the eviction is carried out to completion, a representative of the court will oversee the changing of the locks and the removal of all personal property and possessions from the house to the curb.

- If the bank ends up with the property, its REO department will get the house ready to be sold. Some banks simply hire a Realtor to put the house on the market in "as is" condition. Others fix up the property and sell it for market value. Some banks have in-house property management and real estate operations that dispose of the home.

How to find and acquire properties facing foreclosure

To acquire foreclosed properties, there are different strategies you may want to employ, depending upon the laws in your area. For example, because foreclosure properties in Michigan are subject to a redemption period, investors there can acquire property by working deals with homeowners from the moment they first learn about the upcoming foreclosure until well after the home is sold at the foreclosure auction. Additionally, in states with a redemption period, the Sheriff's Deed or Trustee's Deed that represents the interest purchased in a foreclosure property by the high bidder at the auction becomes a type of paper that can be bought and sold by banks and investors during the redemption period.

If, however, your state has no redemption period, developing methods of discovering impending foreclosures other than simply following the published legal notices becomes vital if you want to make deals directly with homeowners, because they will be cut out of the transaction as soon as the auction is over.

So, as you go through this section of the book, keep in mind that there isn't nearly enough time or space for me to share every possible foreclosure investment strategy with you here. With an open mind, a little creativity, and some experience, you will develop corollaries to my ideas as well as your own methods of generating profits.

Getting the Information You Need

Your first step is to get a firm understanding of the exact foreclosure procedure followed in your area. Your county's Register of Deeds office should be able to fill you in on much of the foreclosure process, or at least point you in the direction of someone who can. If that doesn't get you anywhere, there are always Realtors, attorneys who specialize in real estate, and title companies that may be able to help. When you do locate someone with knowledge of your area's foreclosure process, here are some questions you can ask:

- Where are the foreclosure notices published? How many times is each notice published before the actual foreclosure auction takes place?
- Is there any place you know of where I can find out what properties are going into foreclosure before the notices are published?
- Where are the auctions held and who conducts them? Are they held on a set day and time or just scheduled at the convenience of whoever conducts them?
- Are there standard terms of sale for each auction? If so, what are they?
- Does this state have a statutory redemption period following the sale? If yes, how long is it? If no, when can an investor legally take possession of the home?
- What types of liens are wiped away by the foreclosure auction? Which types are not?
- Are IRS and state income tax liens treated any differently from other liens?

- Where can I do a title search on the properties going to sale?
- What happens to any "overbid" at an auction? (An overbid is any money the successful purchaser bids above and beyond what is owed to the bank.)
- Who handles evictions when former homeowners refuse to leave the property after it is sold? How long does an eviction take?

Tracking Opportunities

Once you've gotten your answers, it's time to begin tracking the foreclosures in your area. All of your research will be conducted with the intent of buying the properties at the foreclosure auction even though you should also be making serious efforts to purchase properties before the sale from homeowners and following the sale from banks.

It stands to reason that you will have less competition from other investors if you begin networking with people in a position to tip you off on potential properties before the foreclosure notices are published. There are many professionals in real estate and related industries who regularly come across this kind of information. If you play your cards right, you can have these people feeding their leads right to you. Following are some of the people you'll want to approach and some suggestions for building relationships with each group:

- Realtors—the most obvious group. People in foreclosure often turn to real estate agents for advice on how to stop the foreclosure and sell their homes. Because most Realtors works on commission, the best way to get their attention is to show them how they can make money by dealing with you.

For example, if an agent refers a foreclosure property to you that you end up buying, you can move toward solidifying the relationship by paying him or her a commission on the purchase and allowing that salesperson to list the property when you put it back on the market.

• Attorneys—They represent both banks and borrowers. Some banks will allow the lawyer handling their foreclosures to work with investors that have a track record putting deals together. A foreclosure can be an expensive proposition for a financial institution, so they may welcome the opportunity to have their lien paid off before the process moves too far along.

Attorneys who handle probate, bankruptcies, and divorces regularly have clients who are on the road toward foreclosure. The key when dealing with lawyers is to remember that they are going to look first and foremost at what course of action will most benefit their client. If you frame your presentation to them in that light, so that selling the property to you becomes a viable and favorable alternative for escaping the foreclosure, most attorneys will at least present that option to their clients.

• Bankers—Why go through the middleman attorney when you can go straight to the source? As I just mentioned, many bankers like the idea of getting delinquent mortgages paid off before going through the foreclosure process. While a person who buys single-family homes in one marketplace is probably too small a player for a national bank to deal with, you can develop relationships with key people at local and regional banks. These institutions keep a much closer eye on any mortgage notes they service themselves. If they view you as a significant player who can help them get paid off on their bad paper, they may be willing to feed you the names of people in trouble.

• Mortgage Brokers—People facing foreclosure often seek to refinance their existing mortgage or take out a second or third one as a way to get the money they need to remedy the situation. Obviously, if people are already behind in their mortgage payments, it is highly unlikely that they will be able to secure a new note or second one. There are mortgage brokers who specialize in financing people facing foreclosure. Keep your eyes and ears open for these individuals because the really good ones can often provide you with more leads than you can handle. Like Realtors, most mortgage people work on commission. So money talks. You may want to offer these salespeople finder's fees for any foreclosure leads they give you that turn into actual acquisitions. Just make sure that it is legal in your state to offer that type of payment to them.

- Condo/Homeowner Associations—These groups know what's going on in their complex or neighborhood. All of the gossip filters through them. Plus, because they are usually responsible for collecting association dues, they will be one of the first groups to know when a homeowner has stopped paying his mortgage, because the association fees normally stop being paid long before the mortgage note goes into default. This means that they often have advance notice of a homeowner's coming financial problems.

Appeal to their desire for a family atmosphere in their neighborhood. Let them know that if you buy any foreclosure properties, you'll rent or sell them to good families who will add to the quality of life there. Remind them that if the first mortgage is sold at a foreclosure auction, any back association dues owed by the delinquent homeowner will most likely be wiped away by the sale. If, however, you work out a deal with the homeowner before the sale, to get clear title to the property you would have to pay off any back association fees.

Building Key Relationships

In addition to contacting people who can refer you to foreclosure leads, you can appeal directly to the homeowners themselves by using advertisements and flyers that explain what you do. A classified ad in your local newspaper can easily generate tons of leads. It could read something like this:

FACING FORECLOSURE?

You don't have to lose all of the equity you've built up in your home just because you've been hit by some hard times. You do have options. **Call Homesavers at 810-555-1234** so we can discuss them. Don't wait until it's too late. Call us now and put the foreclosure nightmare behind you.

Some people are resistant to the idea of selling their home until it's too late. By not coming right out and saying in your ad that you're hoping to buy their home, you can get your foot in the door. This will allow you to meet the people, develop rapport, and get a chance to look inside the house. Before you explain that you buy homes, give them some details about how the foreclosure process works. Emphasize the date when they will lose their home if they decide to do nothing. If they're considering bankruptcy, refer them to a bankruptcy attorney. If they seem interested in refinancing or going after a second mortgage, provide them with the names of some mortgage brokers.

These referrals accomplish two objectives. First, they show these other professionals that you are trying to send business their way. That will make them more receptive to the idea of sending referrals your way in the future. Second, they will show the homeowners that you are actually trying to help them. Even if they decide not to sell to you at your first meeting, keep in touch with them as the foreclosure progresses. Eventually they will have to do something or lose their home. When they come to that realization, if they see that selling their property is the only option available, they will be more likely to give you—someone they trust—the chance to make an offer. If they continue to do nothing and the home goes to foreclosure auction, you will have an edge over other investors because you will know the condition inside the property.

Using Foreclosure Notices

Even as you create marketing programs and build relationships that deliver foreclosure leads to you before they get published, foreclosure notices will likely remain your main source of information. Such notices are almost always published on a county-by-county basis, either in the local paper in small counties or in the publication put out by and for the legal profession in larger counties. Familiarize yourself with the advertising format used in your area by subscribing to the publications that contain your county's foreclosure adver-

Sample Foreclosure Listing

THIS FIRM IS A DEBT COLLECTOR ATTEMPTING TO COLLECT A DEBT. ANY INFORMATION WE OBTAIN WILL BE USED FOR THAT PURPOSE.

MORTGAGE SALE—Default has been made in the conditions of a mortgage made by John Q. Public and Stacy V. Public, Husband and Wife[1] (original mortgagors) to State Federal Savings Bank[2], a Federal Savings Bank, Mortgagee, dated July 14, 1995, and recorded on July 31, 1995 in Liber 06712, on Page 389, Macomb County Records, on which mortgage there is claimed to be due at the date hereof the sum of SIXTY-FOUR THOUSAND ONE HUNDRED NINETY-EIGHT AND 93/100 dollars ($64,198.93)[3], including interest at 7.375% per annum[4].

Under the power of sale contained in said mortgage and the statute in such case made and provided, notice is hereby given that said mortgage will be foreclosed by a sale of the mortgaged premises, or some part of them, at public venue, at the North Main Street entrance to the Macomb County Court Building in the city of Mount Clemens, Macomb County, Michigan, at 10:00 AM on November 5, 1999[5].

Said premises are situated in CITY OF WARREN, Macomb County, Michigan, and are described as:

Lot 83, T. Bogdonovich Farms, as recorded In Liber 32, Page 12 of Plats, Macomb County Records[6]

The redemption period shall be 6 months from the date of such sale[7], unless determined abandoned in accordance with 1948CL 600.3241a, in which case the redemption period shall be 30 days from the date of such sale.

Dated: October 1, 1999

STATE FEDERAL SAVINGS BANK
Mortgagee
James J. Lawyer & Associates, P.C.[8]
ATTORNEY FOR: Mortgagee
4233 North Main Street
Warren, Michigan 48093

tisements. Chances are it will look something like the advertisement shown here, which is based on the foreclosure notices posted in my marketplace in Southeastern Michigan.

The following information is contained in most foreclosure listings, although advertisements in your marketplace may contain more, less, or different data:

1. Name of the mortgagor
2. Name of the mortgagee
3. Amount owed on the mortgage
4. Interest rate of loan
5. Mortgage sale date
6. Legal description of property
7. Length of the property's redemption period, if applicable
8. The mortgage company's attorney

Any vital information that's not contained in the foreclosure notice has to be researched elsewhere. Fortunately, all of the information you need is public record. After you figure out what information you'll need, the best place to start looking is at your county's Register of Deeds office. You may have to manually look through the records there or they may be able to help you locate privately published abstracts and software that can make your research faster and easier. Realtors, attorneys, and title companies may also have access to tools that could help make your research more efficient.

Contacting the Homeowners

Once you've collected your data, there are several ways to make contact with the homeowners. The easiest is to simply send a letter or flyer to the house. As we discussed earlier, it is best to be a little vague at first, much like the preceding classified ad, so that you can at least get in the door, get a look at the property, and start developing some rapport. The only problem with this is that once the foreclosure notices are published, there are almost surely other investors trying to do the same things as you. If you mail letters, the delay between publication of the notice and delivery of your information could provide your competition with all the time they need to steal the deal right out from under you. You could look up the homeowners' phone numbers and try to call them by phone. This certainly could allow you to make contact more quickly; however, there are two problems with this plan. First, it is much too easy for someone to simply hang up on you before you have a chance to complete your sales pitch, especially when you're calling families who are most likely being hounded by collections telemarketers. Second, as I mentioned earlier, many people in foreclosure have already had their phone disconnected by the time their financial problems become public information. The solution, in my opinion, is to get out and knock on their doors so you can speak to people face-to-face and be the first investor on the scene. If this seems a little intimidating, you could still beat your competition to the punch by hand delivering your flyer or letter the same day the notices are published.

When visiting properties to knock on doors and/or drop off flyers, bring along your camera and take plenty of photos. Take notes about the condition of the house. If you get inside, take photos and notes on the interior condition. This is valuable data that will help you determine your top purchase price. Go back to Chapter 5 and review the part about how to evaluate property and determine your purchase price. Those techniques will apply to any single-family homes you consider purchasing.

Using Junior Liens to Your Advantage

When dealing with foreclosures, there is one tool you have that could make the difference between passing on a deal and making a nice profit on it. But you can use this tool only when buying properties directly from the homeowners. In most states all liens that are junior to the one sold at auction are wiped away following the foreclosure sale. This means that as the clock ticks down toward the foreclosure auction (or the end of the redemption period if there is one), not only is the homeowner's interest in the property at risk, but any lien holder in a position junior to the mortgage being sold is also looking at the possibility of having his interest in the house wiped away. The only way these junior lien holders can protect their interest is by going to the foreclosure sale and bidding up the property until they own it or any overbid covers their interest in the property. Sure, some junior lien holders with a large stake in a house might go this route, but the large majority of them simply choose to write off the loss rather than throwing more good money after bad. Knowing this gives you an advantage when making an offer on a property with multiple liens on it that is headed toward foreclosure. Because junior lien holders in this scenario are at serious risk of losing everything once the foreclosure is completed, they will often be willing to release or assign their liens to an investor at a deep discount in an attempt to get at least some of their money back before the lien is wiped away. So, once you have a clear picture of all the liens on the property's title, you may be in a better position than you think to buy the property before the foreclosure auction. We'll cover this area of investment more in-depth in the next chapter.

CHOOSING THE RIGHT PROPERTIES

As you review your property research leading up to the foreclosure auction, certain homes will begin catching your attention based on positive spread between the value of the lien going to sale and the value of the property. As the sale approaches, make every effort to get inside these properties so you can do a proper evaluation. In many cases, though, you will have to make a decision on whether or not to bid based solely on the home's outside appearance. Here are a few tips to keep you from overspending:

- The outside condition of the house will normally give you a good idea of what kind of shape the inside is in. If the windows are cracked, the gutters are falling off, the screen door is dangling on one hinge, and the grass hasn't been mowed in weeks, it's a safe bet that the inside of the property is in a state of disrepair that is similar or worse.
- Always figure that the house will need new paint and carpet throughout. That way, if you're wrong, money is added to your spread, not taken away from it.
- The older the property, the more likely there will be problems with major systems such as heating and cooling, electrical, and plumbing. Plan for a significant amount of unexpected expenses on older homes.
- Be extremely wary of brand new homes that have gone into foreclosure before anyone even lived in them. If a builder goes belly-up and loses a property, it can look terrific on the outside and be unfinished on the inside. You don't want to buy a

property and find that subcontractors who hadn't been paid for their services have removed the furnace, hot water tank, and duct work.

- Talk to the neighbors. Ask them if they've been inside the house. Find out what they know about the interior condition and what they like and dislike about the home.

The Importance of a Title Search

When buying properties at the sale, it is especially important that you thoroughly research the property's title before making any bids. The people conducting the sale have absolutely no obligation to tell you anything about the property other than what is published in the foreclosure notice. And, because banks regularly foreclose on second and third liens as well as primary mortgages, you can quickly find yourself in a world of trouble if you aren't careful with your research. As I mentioned earlier, in most cases all liens that are junior to the one sold at auction are wiped away following the foreclosure sale. That means that if a second mortgage is sold at auction, the primary mortgage remains after the sale is complete. It is NOT wiped away. If you've purchased that second mortgage, the first lien then becomes your responsibility—you can't gain clear title to the property until that primary mortgage is paid off. Hopefully you can see how sloppy research could quite literally cost you thousands upon thousands of dollars. Make certain you know what you're bidding on. If your research leaves you unsure, get the professional opinion of someone knowledgeable in title matters or simply avoid the property.

Familiarize Yourself with the Auction Environment

I suggest that you go to a few foreclosure auctions and watch the proceedings before actually bidding on any properties. Get a feel for how the auctioneer operates and ask him or her about the terms of sale at the auction. Is money due at the sale itself? If not, how soon after the sale is it due? Do you have to pay with certified funds or will a personal check work? Watch other investors to see how they operate. Do they have any telltale voice inflections or mannerisms that give away when they're going to stop bidding? In what size increments does the bidding move when two investors compete for the same property?

Preset Your Maximum Bid

The more you observe during your preliminary visits to the auctions, the better off you'll be when you finally do have a property to bid on at the sale. When that day arrives, make sure you show up at the foreclosure auction with a set price that you'd be willing to spend on the property. I've been to enough auctions to know that it is very easy to get carried away when the bidding starts on a property you want. If you've decided the maximum amount you'll pay and written it down someplace where nobody but you can look at it during the bidding, you'll be less likely to be swept up into a bidding war. Once another investor bids the price above your maximum, simply stop bidding and let the property go. A good side effect of this strategy is that it will allow you to keep a poker face that won't tip other investors off to what you're thinking about. If you enter the bidding already knowing what your maximum bid will be, as the price rises, you can calmly and quickly state your bid without all of the hemming and hawing characteristic of investors who show up at the sale not knowing how much they're willing to spend on a property. This gives you an edge, because other investors will have no idea of when you're going to stop bidding, while you can easily see when the unprepared investors are approaching their ceiling, because they'll take more time to think—and possibly even lower their bidding increments—before making a bid.

After going to a few auctions, you may discover that you are not cut out for purchasing property in that type of environment.

Personally, I am a terrible bidder. I hate losing so much that when I have gone to auctions, I would do whatever it took to come home with a property, even if it sometimes meant paying more than I should. After several bad buys I finally realized that I should send someone else to do the bidding. At first this person just went to the sale with a top price and bid up the property until it went beyond that price. Later on, I added key people to my organization who not only did the bidding for me, but also did the research and much of the value-setting leading up to the auction. Joe, my co-author, got started in real estate investment by handling foreclosure auctions for my company. Unlike me, Joe showed a knack for not getting caught up in the emotion of the auction, which made him the perfect person to maximize our profits on those kinds of sales. Since his start with me, Joe has moved to Tennessee and set up his own successful real estate investment operation, which proves you can apply the concepts in this book to just about any part of the country.

Buying from the Highest Bidder

Chances are that some of the properties you research in preparation for auction will get sold back to the financial institution that originally held the lien. The bank will most likely want to get rid of these properties as soon as possible. You will have up to two more chances to bid on any of them. The first one comes immediately following the foreclosure sale, but you have to act quickly. Track down the bank's REO (Real Estate Owned) department and let them know that you'd like to make a cash offer on the property they just took back. You will simply offer them the amount you were willing to pay at the foreclosure sale. If you can catch them before they've put any additional time or money into listing, rehabbing, or otherwise preparing the house for resale, there's a good chance that they will at least consider your offer. Be sure to let them know that you're offering cash and you're prepared to close immediately. Ask questions about how they operate when dealing with repossessed properties. The more specifics you learn about their procedures, the better chance you will have to acquire property directly from them.

If they reject your offer, don't fear; you still have another chance to buy this property. Give the address to your Realtor so he can let you know when the property shows up as a listing in the MLS. Once it's listed, have the agent write a cash offer for the amount you were ready to spend at the foreclosure auction and submit it to the listing agent. If the bank refuses your offer yet again, have your Realtor let the listing agent know that yours is a standing offer that the bank can accept in the future if it is unhappy with the interest the property generates.

There are hot times of the year when you are likely to have more success in buying properties from a bank's REO department—either directly from the bank or through a Realtor who has the house listed. In sales and finance, success is often measured in production numbers that are broken down into annual, quarterly, and monthly figures. As the people in the bank's REO department approach the end of one of these time frames, they will usually be working a little harder trying to make things happen to beef up the given segment's sales figures. So, if you work a little harder near the end of the current month, quarter, or year, you can often get a better deal on an REO property than you would at another time. For example, an offer you make on the fifth of March may be turned down, while that same offer may be accepted on the twenty-fifth of March, when the REO staff is concerned about the sales figures for that quarter.

Summary

As the number of homes at risk of foreclosure increases, so do the opportunities for building wealth through investing in foreclosed properties. And, as such an investor, you can offer a valuable service to homeowners facing the loss of their homes, by giving the opportunity to keep some of the equity they've built up and avoid a foreclosure on their credit records. However, before you begin investing in these properties, it is important that you understand the foreclosure process, the mind-set of homeowners facing it, how the bidding process works, and the rules of your area. Before you bid on a property, be sure to do a comprehensive title search and to find out as much as you can about the condition of the property, and always, always pre-set your maximum bid before you go to auction.

CHAPTER 8

Profiting from Nonperforming Paper

One of the most underappreciated areas of real estate investment is the buying and selling of the actual mortgage notes written on the underlying property, which are known as "paper." Paper is largely ignored because many people are intimidated by the prospect of negotiating with banks. Those who are making money at it don't mind if the rest of us believe that investing in paper is a highly complicated business. In reality, the concepts that underlie investing in paper are quite simple, and if you do your homework properly, you can virtually lock a minimum level of profit into such deals.

There are many investors who make a nice profit from writing and buying performing mortgage notes, but those kinds of deals are really more like investing in stocks and bonds than in real estate. For most people who invest in performing paper, actually owning the underlying property is the last thing they want. These investors are much happier, and usually better off, if the borrower simply makes his or her payments on time. If you have an interest in that area of investment, you could probably turn to your stockbroker, accountant, or financial planner for more information. Because this book is about making money by investing in real estate, I want to focus on nonperforming paper—investments that will put you in a position to eventually own the underlying property.

Simply put, nonperforming paper includes mortgages, deeds of trust, and liens that are not being paid on time and/or not being paid in full. When the paper is not performing, that loan is worth less money when sold in the secondary market. The good news for a real estate investor, however, is that you are more interested in the underlying property than the liens on it. If you can negotiate discounted prices for the purchase or release of the nonperforming note, it could allow you to get great deals on the real estate.

Recognizing a good paper deal

As you research foreclosure and tax sale properties, pay special attention to those homes that fit the following characteristics:

- There are two or more liens on the title and the most senior lien is the one foreclosing on the property. The foreclosure gets the ball rolling and forces everyone in a junior position to make a decision. Do they pay off the foreclosing lien to protect their own position or do they do nothing and watch their lien simply disappear? For the junior lien holders, the ideal scenario would be for an investor to show up and try to purchase their position. (I assume you see where I'm going with this line of thinking.)
- The homeowner is losing the property because of taxes. As with the preceding scenario, all lien holders in a junior position can benefit from an investor purchasing their position.
- The senior lien is larger than any of the junior liens. A bank holding a second mortgage—a junior lien—is much more likely to step up and buy all of the liens ahead of theirs if their investment in the property is more than the liens in foreclosure. If, however, a bank holds a junior lien for, say $20,000,

while the primary mortgage being foreclosed on is worth $90,000, the second mortgage holder may simply cut its losses on the property and let its position be wiped out. Most banks—except for local financial institutions and those with a strong knowledge of the local real estate market—will not throw more good money after bad. However, the bank can reduce its losses if an investor interested in the property shows up and makes an offer for the bank's position.

- There are multiple liens on the property, but the senior lien alone is not worth more than 70–75 percent of the property's market value. It's okay if all of the liens together add up to more than the house is worth as long as the primary mortgage leaves you a big enough spread to negotiate with the other lien holders and the homeowner.

Timing is everything

Once you know what to look for, you'll start noticing potential nonperforming paper deals as you prepare for foreclosure and tax auctions. There are certainly properties not in foreclosure that might allow you to put together a nonperforming paper deal, but the time pressure of a foreclosure proceeding forcing everyone to either make a deal or lose everything is your most important weapon. A foreclosure—or during the redemption period if your state has one—is the perfect opportunity for an outside investor to step into the picture. As the date approaches when the owner's and all junior lien holders' interest in the property will be lost, everyone will become increasingly willing to put together a transaction that will allow them to at least recoup some portion of their original investments.

If you live in a state with no redemption period on foreclosures, you have to act quickly once you find a property. It takes time to put together a nonperforming paper deal. If your state has a redemption period, you have until the redemption period expires to close this kind of transaction. Even in that case, you'll probably still end up sealing the deal at the last minute, when the time pressure forces everyone to act. However, a key advantage to having a redemption period is that you'll have lots of time to plant the seeds of the deal in the minds of all the players involved.

Prospecting for paper deals

When investing in nonperforming paper, the only way you'll ever have any real success is if you initially deal directly with the homeowner. As an outsider to the situation, you will have a difficult—if not impossible—time securing details about the paper. You will almost always need written authorization from the homeowner in order to discuss details such as principal balance, number of payments behind, payment history, and so on.

Like dealing with normal foreclosures, your best bet for reaching a prospect for a nonperforming paper deal is by knocking on the homeowner's door or hand delivering a letter to the house. (See the sample letter in Chapter 13.) Once you get inside, make it clear that you're looking to purchase their home. Remind them that unless they do something to stop the foreclosure, they will eventually lose their home anyway. By allowing you to work on deals with the junior lien holders, the homeowners are giving themselves a chance to seize control of the situation, possibly avoid the foreclosure, and maybe even put some money in their pockets once the house is sold.

Getting started

When the homeowner agrees to work with you, it is best to get his or her commitment in writing by executing a sales contract that is contingent upon your working out discounts with the junior lien holders. You should work with your real estate attorney to write the contingency language before you approach prospects. If the homeowner is unwilling to sign a deal, don't let that stop you from going forward. He or she may be willing to give you written permission to negotiate with his or her creditors. Once you learn more about the situation, you may discover ways to profit whether the homeowner cooperates or not. The information that you will get from the homeowner can help you make money on the property whether or not the homeowner ultimately decides to sell the house to you. But we'll get to all of that a little bit later.

Working with the Homeowner

Once the homeowner agrees to work with you, request detailed information about each mortgage or lien on the title, including

- The name and address of the company that currently holds the lien
- The names and phone numbers of any contact persons the homeowner's been dealing with at the financial institution
- All account numbers associated with the account
- Copies of any recent statements or correspondence from the lien holder
- The homeowner's estimate of what he or she still owes on the note
- Date and amount of the last payment sent to the bank
- Details on any ongoing disputes or discrepancies with the account

Once you've gathered all of this information, double check its accuracy by reviewing your title search. Make sure there aren't any additional mortgages, back taxes, special tax assessments, fixture filings, mechanic's liens, judgments, or other liens on the title.

Failure to account for a single item on the title could easily kill your deal—or, even worse, destroy your profit margin after the deal is completed.

WORKING WITH THE LIEN HOLDERS

After you're certain that you have a complete list of liens on the property, it's time to start contacting banks. Begin with a simple phone call to each lien holder asking how you go about requesting a payoff amount. Many financial institutions will require the written permission of the homeowner to provide you with information about the property, and most will require you to fax them a payoff letter request that includes the following information:

- Name of the borrower
- Account number
- Property address
- Date of payoff
- Your contact information

When determining the payoff date, I suggest that you use a date that is a minimum of either a month away or the day before the owner loses the home in foreclosure, so that you can have the time you need to negotiate with other lien holders. If you get more than a few days past the payoff date, many financial institutions require you to get a new payoff letter before they will accept your money and release the lien. Once the payoff expires, any discounts you have negotiated can be withdrawn by the bank. There's nothing more frustrating than negotiating discounts with two or three lenders only to have one kill your deal at the last minute by having second thoughts after the payoff has expired.

Once the bank receives your written payoff request, they may present you with a payoff figure over the phone, but ask that the payoff letter be faxed to you. The payoff letter you receive from the bank will include the total due to retire that note on the date you specified and the amount in interest payments that will be added to the payoff for each day it is delayed.

When the payoff letters start coming in, organize your information as presented in the following example.

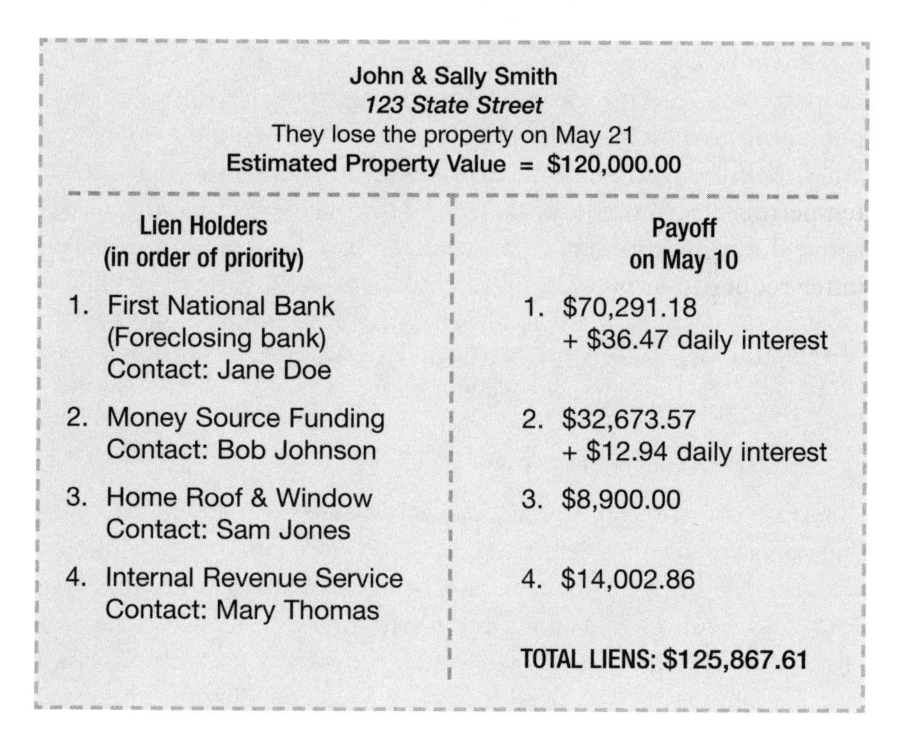

John & Sally Smith
123 State Street
They lose the property on May 21
Estimated Property Value = $120,000.00

Lien Holders (in order of priority)	Payoff on May 10
1. First National Bank (Foreclosing bank) Contact: Jane Doe	1. $70,291.18 + $36.47 daily interest
2. Money Source Funding Contact: Bob Johnson	2. $32,673.57 + $12.94 daily interest
3. Home Roof & Window Contact: Sam Jones	3. $8,900.00
4. Internal Revenue Service Contact: Mary Thomas	4. $14,002.86
	TOTAL LIENS: $125,867.61

Determining payoff offers

Using the preceding example of John and Sally Smith, let's take a look at how to proceed once you receive the payoff amounts from the lien holders. Begin by figuring out how much you should offer for the house. Let's say the property is in relatively good shape and that, after figuring in repairs, interest expense, closing costs, commissions, and your spread, you decide that you would be willing to spend $93,000 to acquire this home. Now, using that number, you have to figure out what to offer each financial institution for their position. When it comes to negotiating discounts, the general rule of thumb is that the lower the position of the lien, the bigger the discount the lien holder would be willing to consider.

The Primary Mortgage Holder

In our example, it's a waste of time trying to squeeze any discount out of the primary lien holder. In some cases—usually when the amount mortgaged is higher than the value of the underlying property—a first mortgage may be willing to consider a discounted payoff, but not in this one. The primary lien holder is in a strong position, because the mortgaged amount is well below the property value. So about $70,300 is already tied up in that single payoff. That leaves you with $22,700 to divide among the other liens.

Junior Lien Holders

After the primary lien holder, you should contact the IRS, because the government tends to take the longest to respond and negotiate. To find the proper contact person at the IRS, start by calling your local IRS field office and ask them whom you can contact regarding real estate liens. In this case, with the IRS in fourth position, I would simply ask the representative to consider releasing their lien from the property when the title changes hands. With all of the obligations stacked up in front of them, it is highly unlikely that they would ever receive any overbid money from the foreclosure auction. It is equally unlikely that the IRS would be willing to pay nearly $112,000 to protect their $14,000 position. And, because they can easily attach their lien to any other real estate or personal property owned by John and Sally Smith, there's a good chance they'll agree to a release without any payment. Remember, the IRS stands to have its lien wiped out anyway if the property goes to foreclosure. Even if the government agrees to a discount or a release, they will still go after the Smiths for the balance owed.

While you're waiting for the IRS to respond (and you hope send a written acknowledgment of their intent to release), you should be making calls to the second and third lien holders. At larger banks, you will probably need to track down a decision maker through the foreclosure or loss mitigation department. At smaller banks, ask for the person who handles the buying and selling of mortgages. With a home improvement company, start with the owner or manager and let them work with you or direct you to someone who can put a deal together.

As you deal with each of these lien holders, it's important to explain that you're trying to put a deal together (it's helpful to have a signed purchase agreement to show them), but that it will work only if all the lien holders fall in line. Small businesses, like the roof and window company in our example, are the wild card in these deals. Even though they are in a tenuous position, they may be the most difficult to negotiate with. When you're dealing with the government or a bank, most of the time you negotiate with an employee who has no personal interest in the transaction. From this detached viewpoint, the negotiator can take an unbiased look at the facts of the situation and make a decision based on what logically makes sense for the company. When dealing with smaller companies, you're much more likely to run into a business owner who has his or her own money tied up in the lien. There may even be an unpleasant history between the business owner and the homeowner because of collection attempts. Someone in this position is much more likely to let emotions interfere with business sense.

When talking to the home improvement company, explain the facts. Again, based on the example of the Smiths, you can say, "This property is scheduled for foreclosure, and all junior liens will be wiped away on May 21. Your company is sitting in third position with a relatively small interest in the property. You have a few options. You could pony up about $103,000, pay off the two mortgages ahead of you and then foreclose on the property yourself. Of course, that would mean your money would be tied up for months and you would incur the additional expense of the foreclosure. Or, you could do nothing and most likely watch your lien be wiped out. Or, you could work with me to put this deal together so that I can help you at least recoup some portion of your investment."

Start by offering about $2,000, but quickly add that you may have to come back for a bigger discount if the second mortgage holder isn't willing to bend. This will underscore your point that, being in third position, this lien holder is likely to lose everything, thus adding appeal to the opportunity to at least recoup $2,000.

PROFITING FROM ASSIGNMENT OF THE MORTGAGE NOTE

The bank in second position should be handled a little differently from the others. As you did with the other lien holders, start by explaining that you're looking for a discounted release so you can put the deal together, but then add that you'd be willing to put up the money right now if the bank agrees to sell you an assignment of their note at a discount. Buying an assignment means instead of releasing the note, ownership of the debt is transferred to you. The borrowers now owe you the payoff amount of $32,867.61, and you now sit in second position on the title. Getting an assignment puts you in a powerful position, because you are now in the deal whether the homeowner sells to you or not. To illustrate how this works, let's get back to the example of the Smiths. Assuming the third position accepts your offer of $2,000, and the IRS releases its lien of $14,000, you have about $21,000 left to spend on the second note. If the bank agrees to accept that for a release, you can then close the deal and take title to the house. If, however, the bank is willing to sell you an assignment for the $21,000, the game changes a little. You can now afford to spend most of the $2,000 you offered the home improvement company on the assignment of the second mortgage. That's because the assignment puts you in a perfect position to make money on the property at the foreclosure sale even if some other investor outbids you for the property.

Let's say that you bought an assignment of the second mortgage for $21,000. When this property goes on the auction block at the foreclosure sale, the bidding will start somewhere near the payoff amount of $70,291.18. To keep the math simple, let's say the bidding opens at $71,000. Once that opening bid is read, you could immediately bid $103,600 on the property, because you own the $32,673.57 debt of the second lien. If anyone else bids against you—which is unlikely in this case—let them have the house. I'll explain the method to my madness.

You already own the second mortgage, which you purchased for a total of $21,000, but the mortgage has a payoff value of a little over $32,600. As you will recall from the discussion of overbids in Chapter 7, as the second lien holder, you are entitled to collect any overbid amount up to the total payoff of your lien. So, by bidding $103,600, you guarantee yourself an overbid of $32,600. If nobody bids against you, you end up owning the house. In that case, you would pay the $103,600 of your winning bid, but as a lien holder, you can immediately apply to collect the $32,600 of overbid you are due. So, you are actually buying the property for the $21,000 you originally paid for the second lien assignment plus the $71,000 required to pay off the primary lien, or a total investment of $92,000. If, however, another investor bids against you on the property, you can let him have it and still collect a nice profit. When he or she buys the property, you can still apply for the $32,600 overbid, which means that you would make a profit of $11,600 just for injecting yourself into the deal by buying the assignment to the second mortgage. And, since junior liens are wiped out by the foreclosure auction, the third and fourth position lien holders lose their stake in the property unless they bid more than you.

VARIATIONS ON A THEME

The more you get into nonperforming paper deals, the more variations and possible outcomes you'll encounter. Just looking at the preceding example, you could have tried to negotiate a slightly lower price for the second lien assignment and then bought an assignment of the third lien. Or once you owned the second lien, you could have approached the primary lien holder about buying an assignment of his or her position, which could save you money on interest, penalties, and fees tacked onto the payoff and the foreclosure bid price.

Summary

The buying and selling of the actual mortgage notes written on the underlying property, which are known as "paper," is one of the most underappreciated areas of real estate investment. The best way to succeed with these transactions is by dealing directly with the homeowner. When working with lien holders, keep in mind that, generally, the lower the position of the lien holder, the greater the discount they should be willing to accept. The more you work with nonperforming paper deals, the more you'll see that there are many ways to handle each one, so if you enjoy a challenge, you will love working on these kinds of transactions.

CHAPTER 9

Cashing in on Government and Secondary Mortgage Market Foreclosures

Back in the early days of the twentieth century, homeownership was a status achieved only by the very wealthy or the very frugal who went without all but the basic necessities for years until they had the funds required to buy a house. Down payment requirements were typically 35 percent or more of the purchase price. Mortgages usually had to be paid off in less than 10 years, and they were often structured so that the borrower paid just interest until the loan expired, at which time a balloon payment of the entire principal was due. With such stringent financial guidelines, few people could afford to buy a home, and of those who did, many defaulted on their mortgages.

Mortgage terms remained much the same as the United States headed into the Roaring Twenties, but the number of homeowners steadily rose as people took advantage of the huge profits being reaped on Wall Street. The real estate market flourished until Black Tuesday, October 29, 1929, when the stock market collapse wiped out millions of dollars in "paper" profits in a single day. The standard structure of home mortgages doomed the average

American to default when the balloon payment came due. As the Great Depression tightened its grip on the U.S. economy, millions of families lost their homes.

New government programs and agencies

As a result of the catastrophic losses of millions of homeowners after the stock market crash of the late twenties, and the often insurmountable barriers to home ownership posed by mortgage terms, the federal government stepped in, creating new opportunities for Americans to purchase their own homes.

FHA and Fannie Mae

Prospective home buyers got a huge boost when Congress created the Federal Housing Administration (FHA) through the National Housing Act of 1934. The government's objective was to spur lenders to write long-term, fixed-rate mortgages so more Americans could afford to become homeowners. FHA provided insurance that protected financial institutions when borrowers defaulted on these types of loans. Four years later, in response to banks' concerns that writing and holding long-term mortgages would dry up their working capital, Congress created the Federal National Mortgage Association (FNMA), known as Fannie Mae. This corporation, which was wholly owned by the federal government, created a secondary market for residential mortgages. Fannie Mae began buying FHA-insured loans, which allowed banks to write more mortgages and recycle their money more regularly. This opened the door for more Americans to become homeowners. Then, in 1944, when Congress passed the Serviceman's Readjustment Act, which gave the Department of Veterans Affairs the ability to guarantee zero-down mortgages to veterans, the floodgates opened. Soldiers returning home from World War II could become homeowners with little or no up-front investment. Fannie Mae's authority was expanded so it could now also purchase these new Veterans Administration (VA) loans.

Ginnie Mae and Freddie Mac

As a result of the government programs of the 1930s, 1940s, and 1950s, the real estate market boomed and owning a home became an integral part of the American Dream. Then, in the late 1960s and early 1970s, Congress added to the secondary mortgage market by creating the Government National Mortgage Association (GNMA), or Ginnie Mae, and the Federal Home Loan Mortgage Corporation (FHLMC), or Freddie Mac. The FHA was absorbed into the newly formed Department of Housing and Urban Development (HUD). A Cabinet-level federal agency, HUD was created to develop national policy and programs that address America's housing needs. Fannie Mae became a private organization, which allowed it to purchase conventional mortgages as well as FHA and VA loans. Freddie Mac was also set up as a private corporation and immediately began focusing its purchasing on conventional loans. Ginnie Mae, an agency of HUD, became the only remaining agency owned by the government. Ginnie Mae purchases only government insured and guaranteed loans.

A Boom in Homeownership

The creation and continued development of the secondary mortgage market has made a huge impact on real estate. Lenders could turn their money over faster, allowing them to write more loans and make bigger profits. FHA and VA loans significantly lowered the barriers to entry into the homeowner club and transformed the idea of purchasing a house from an unattainable dream for all but the wealthy in the early part of the 1900s to something that nearly every American can achieve today.

New opportunities for real estate investors

As you may have guessed, the birth and growth of the secondary mortgage market has also created new opportunities for real estate investors. All of these organizations—Fannie Mae, Ginnie Mae, and Freddie Mac—own huge amounts of residential mortgages, and the FHA and VA insure and guarantee billions of dollars in loans. With all of those mortgages pooled in so few places, even a small percentage of defaults will result in large numbers of foreclosed-upon properties owned by a few organizations. All of these secondary market players—and some other government agencies, such as the Internal Revenue Service—have inventories of properties they sell to the general public. If you can learn the ins and outs of each group's bidding procedure, this is a terrific source for properties to acquire for renting or flipping.

When a bank-owned FHA-insured or VA-guaranteed mortgage goes into foreclosure, the bank follows the normal foreclosure process we discussed in Chapter 7. However, once the foreclosure auction is over, HUD or the VA pays the bank the balance owed on the loan and takes possession of the property.

Because FHA and VA loans require little or no down payment, they have a higher foreclosure rate than other loans. There are several reasons for this. People who make a large down payment on their home create instant equity for themselves that can often be pulled out of the house in times of need to bring a delinquent mortgage current. Additionally, those who don't have a large financial investment in their home don't have so much to lose by simply walking away when faced with foreclosure. Finally, as it gets easier to get into a home with less money coming out of their pockets, many people jump in without realizing the level of financial commitment necessary to be homeowners. Inevitably, poor money management or some outside financial crisis leads to their downfall. So, when FHA-insured and VA-guaranteed properties go through foreclosure, there is usually little or no equity in them, which means that they will not generate interest from the average investor at the foreclosure auction. When HUD and the VA get these houses back, they list them at "market value" and attempt to sell them to the public.

Like bank Real Estate Owned (REO) properties, when these properties hit the market, you should have already completed some research on them if you've been tracking foreclosures long enough. The good news is that now you can actually get a look inside the homes you couldn't get into while getting ready for the foreclosure auction.

Because Ginnie Mae purchases only loans insured or guaranteed by the government, foreclosure properties it gets back are normally returned to the appropriate federal agency, which then pays Ginnie Mae the balance owed on the mortgage.

Like Ginnie Mae, Fannie Mae and Freddie Mac return foreclosed FHA and VA loans to the corresponding government agency. Because they also purchase uninsured conventional loans, these two organizations wind up owning properties when these types of loans go into default.

Preparing to invest in government and secondary market foreclosures

In disposing of foreclosed properties, the steps taken by each government and secondary mortgage organization vary. The following are some details about how each organization goes about disposing of the homes it acquires.

HUD PROPERTIES

All HUD houses are listed with Realtors on the local Multiple Listing Service (MLS). Investors must use a real estate agent to get inside the properties and to submit offers. HUD accepts bids on a property during an "Offer Period" when the property is first put on the market. When the offer period is completed, bids are opened and the home is basically sold to the highest bidder, although HUD does give priority to bids by prospective owner occupants over investors. You can bid on properties not sold during the offer period on any business day. HUD does not offer any financing to prospective buyers.

You can find out more about the process as well as what properties HUD has for sale by visiting its web site at www.hud.gov.

VA foreclosures

Sales of VA foreclosures are handled in a similar manner to HUD homes. They are listed on the local MLS by area Realtors who can grant prospective buyers access to the properties. The VA also gives priority to bids by prospective owner occupants over investors. Unlike HUD, the VA also offers seller financing on most properties at competitive rates with a modest down payment.

Details about many VA foreclosure properties can be found online at www.homeloans.va.gov/homes.htm. Regional VA offices manage the sales. Those that don't list properties on the web usually advertise them in local newspapers. Your best bet is to go to the website, find the regional office that services your area, and contact them for more information.

Fannie Mae properties

Fannie Mae also lists its repossessed properties with local Realtors on the MLS. It operates much like banks that market their REO homes in this manner.

You can get more information about Fannie Mae and access a list of available properties at www.fanniemae.com.

Freddie Mac properties

Freddie Mac has created an arm to the organization called HomeSteps. The sole purpose of HomeSteps is to divest Freddie

Mac of properties it acquires. Unlike the preceding organizations, most HomeSteps houses have been repaired and renovated. As an investor, you may want to first look at the homes they are selling in "as is" condition for your best chances to find undervalued properties. HomeSteps also offers "Special Financing" on their sales with down payments as low as 5 percent, although it may be more difficult for an investor to take advantage of that type of program if he or she isn't planning on living in the house.

You can learn more about Freddie Mac at www.freddiemac.com. You can research available properties at www.homesteps.com.

Other Foreclosure Investment Sources

In addition to the major players described here, there are additional organizations and government agencies that regularly acquire and sell residential property. The following is a list of these groups and their websites, where you can find more information and individual property details:

- Internal Revenue Service (IRS)—www.treas.gov/auctions
- Federal Deposit Insurance Corporation (FDIC)—www.fdic.gov
- Small Business Administration (SBA)—www.sba.gov
- U.S. Army Corps of Engineers—www.sas.usace.army.mil/hapinv
- U.S. General Services Administration (GSA)—www.propertydisposal.gsa.gov

With a little research you can also uncover agencies of your local, county, and state governments that provide financing to home buyers. In short, any organization or government agency that lends money to home buyers or purchases mortgages in the secondary market will eventually end up owning properties through foreclosures. Each of them is likely to have different systems in place for disposing of the houses they acquire. By learning as much as you can about their processes and developing relationships with the people within the organization who oversee the sale of properties, you can create many opportunities for yourself to acquire quality real estate at or below market value.

Summary

The growth of the secondary mortgage market has made a huge impact on real estate. Most significantly, FHA and VA loans dramatically lowered the barriers to homeownership. But along with this increase in homeownership, the birth and growth of the secondary mortgage market has also created new opportunities for real estate investors. All of the organizations, such as Fannie Mae, Ginnie Mae, and Freddie Mac, and some other government agencies, such as the Internal Revenue Service, have inventories of properties they sell to the general public. Learn the rules of each group's bidding procedure, and you'll be able to tap into an excellent source for properties to acquire for renting or flipping.

CHAPTER 10

Tax Sales Can Help You Achieve Your Goals

Along with the benefits of owning property comes the important responsibility of paying property taxes. Property tax revenue normally remains in the local community to help fund school budgets as well as local and countywide services. A tax assessor or commissioner, who is a part of the county government, normally handles collection of these funds. Because of the important role property taxes play in the local economy, the law has been set up to hand out severe penalties to those who do not pay their taxes. What this means to real estate investors is that those who are willing to put their money up to cover the delinquent taxes stand to benefit by earning the interest and penalties charged to the homeowner. If the property owner never pays the back taxes, interest, and penalties, the investor can eventually take title to the property. Because property tax laws vary greatly by state, I'm providing some general concepts in this chapter. It is very important that you investigate your local laws, regulations, and procedures before investing real money in this area.

Investing in delinquent property taxes

Putting your capital into delinquent property tax instruments can be among the most lucrative—and safest—investments you'll ever find. In almost all cases, unpaid property taxes take the first lien position on the title of a property no matter how encumbered the property may be. Put another way, this means that delinquent property taxes can never be wiped away by the foreclosure of any lien—including IRS and state tax liens. They must be paid before clear title to a property can pass from one owner to the next, and when delinquent property taxes are sold to an outside investor and any applicable redemption period is allowed to expire, they can wipe away all other liens. That means all other liens can be eliminated if the owner of the junior paper in question does not step forward to protect his position by bidding at the tax sale. So, basically, when you own a delinquent property tax instrument, you're in the driver's seat with a first-position interest in the property.

How tax sales are handled

Because unpaid property taxes represent lost revenue, many counties go out of their way to help those who generate revenue for the county by investing in tax deeds or liens. When you put your money up to buy a delinquent tax instrument, you are providing a revenue stream for the local government and taking away a potential expense for them at the same time. There has been a movement across the country in the last decade or so to make these kinds of investments easier and more profitable for the average person to take advantage of. Many states have gone so far as to raise the return on investors' money, shorten the length of redemption periods, hire additional staff to work with potential investors, and take advantage of the Internet and other marketing tools to let people know about the money to be made at tax sales.

In almost every state, tax sales are held by an arm of the county government. There are a few states, such as Texas, where the sales are farmed out to attorneys. In other states—mostly in New England—tax sales are conducted by governments or their representatives at the town or city level. No matter who holds the sales, however, there are two main types of investment vehicles sold at tax sales across the country: tax deeds and tax lien certificates. Each state sells one or the other at the initial tax sale. They do not sell both.

TAX DEEDS VERSUS TAX LIEN CERTIFICATES

If your state is a tax deed state, it means that you are purchasing the actual deed to the property at the tax sale. If there is a redemption period, once it is over, the property is yours. If your state sells tax lien certificates, it is selling you a first-position lien on the property, which means that following any redemption period you must then foreclose on the homeowner to take title to the property. Some states require the same foreclosure process that banks use for run-of-the-mill mortgage foreclosures, while others have modified versions set up especially for tax lien certificates.

There are no hard and fast rules that apply everywhere around the country when it comes to how tax sales are handled. Some general guidelines are as follows: Tax lien certificate states tend to have longer redemption periods than tax deed states. Tax deed states are more likely to charge the property owner a percentage of the outstanding tax paid by the investor as a penalty—meaning that if a homeowner redeems her property on the day following the sale, she will pay the same flat percentage penalty on her back taxes as she would if she redeemed on the last possible day. Conversely, tax lien certificate states are more likely to charge redeeming homeowners per annum interest, meaning that if your state required 12 percent interest to be paid when redeeming tax lien certificates, and you were redeemed in the first month, you would earn just one percent on your money.

Of course, these are broad guidelines that may not apply to your state. There is a very wide range in the terms you may encounter, depending on where you live. For example, I have come across states with interest or penalty rates as low as 5 percent and others as high as 50 percent, and redemption periods that range from none to seven years. And, as I mentioned earlier, these terms are constantly being revised by states that see the benefit of enticing people to invest in their back property taxes.

Be well informed

When you start checking out the tax sales in your county, visit one of these officials or departments if your county has one:

- County Trustee
- Delinquent Tax Department
- County Tax Commissioner
- County Tax Assessor

Once you locate someone who has details about tax sales in your area, here are some questions you should have the answers to before putting any of your money on the line:

- Who conducts the tax sales?
- Where and how often are they held?
- Do you sell tax deeds or tax lien certificates?
- Is there any other interest in the property that could ever have priority over the tax deed or tax lien certificates I buy at the sale, other than prior delinquent taxes?
- When I buy a delinquent property tax instrument, is there anything I must do to protect my position on the title, such as

recording my interest or buying future tax lien certificates on the property as they go to sale?

- Is there any redemption period following the sale? How long is it?
- What percentage of investors would you say get redeemed?
- If there's a redemption period, what is the process I must follow to take possession of the property once the redemption period expires?
- If I buy a tax lien certificate, do I have to foreclose on the homeowner once the redemption period expires?
- If I have to evict the former homeowners, how much will the eviction cost me?
- Are there any legal means by which I can reduce any redemption period?
- Is the homeowner charged interest or a penalty when he or she redeems? If so, what is the percentage rate and how much of that do I receive following the redemption?
- How can I get a list of the properties scheduled for sale?
- What are the purchasing terms on deeds or lien certificates bought at the sale?
- Does the county offer any financing of purchases?
- How does the bidding work?
- Are there any additional costs besides the back taxes? If yes, are those expenses added to the total before the bidding starts or after it's completed?
- What happens to properties that do not sell at the auction? Can I buy them directly from the county? If not, how do I make offers on them? How can I get a list of these properties?

Do your homework before the tax sale auction

Much like foreclosures, as you prepare for tax sales, it's a good idea to contact homeowners before the actual auction to try and work out deals with them before the sale takes place. By working with you, the homeowners have the opportunity to keep the equity they have in the home, as well as avoid foreclosure proceedings. Check with a Realtor to see if any of the properties in which you're interested are listed on the Multiple Listing Service (MLS) so you can get a look inside them before bidding.

As you research your property, you should set your maximum bid based on the maximum amount you'd be willing to pay for that particular house. Even though more than 80 percent of tax deeds and tax lien certificates are redeemed, if you overpay for one of them, you're setting yourself up for trouble. Pay extra attention to properties that have been abandoned, whose owners live out of state, or that serve as the owner's second or vacation home. Homeowners are much more likely not to redeem these kinds of properties than if the back taxes are owed on a primary residence. Stay away from properties that are landlocked, inaccessible, or too small for any development. Also make note of zoning ordinances before bidding on any raw land. The zoning of a particular area could easily make a seemingly valuable parcel of land virtually worthless without a variance. Either get your variance approved in writing ahead of time or strongly consider passing on the property.

Learn the Terminology

Your research will go easier if you can gain an understanding of how to read legal descriptions, because when counties prepare their tax sale lists, properties are usually identified only by their legal descriptions.

There are three primary systems used to describe real estate in the United States:

- Metes and Bounds:

  This system is used mainly in describing rural property. A licensed land surveyor creates the legal description by choosing an easily identifiable starting point and verbally walking the reader around the property using metes—the distances from one point in the description to the next—and bounds—the actual directions from one point to the next.

  Here is an example of a metes and bounds legal description: *Starting at an elm tree on the west side of Hickory Road; thence along Hickory Road in a northwesterly direction for 501 feet to an iron pin; thence in a southwesterly direction for 682 feet along the south fence of the Armstrong farm; thence in a southeasterly direction for 396 feet to an iron pin; thence in a southeasterly direction for 518 feet back to the starting point.*

- Rectangular or Government Survey System:

  Like metes and bounds, the rectangular, or government, survey system is mainly utilized for describing rural or agricultural real estate. However, this system is designed only to measure rectangular- and square-shaped tracts of land. Land is divided by north–south lines called "principal meridians" and east–west lines called "baselines." These principal meridians and baselines are given names to tell them apart. There are additional north–south lines called "range lines" located every six miles east and west of each principal meridian and additional east–west lines called "township lines" located every six miles north and south of each baseline. All of these lines form a huge grid full of boxes that are each six miles long by six miles wide. Each of these boxes is called a "township" and then further divided into 36 sections, each one mile long by one mile wide. These sections are then divided into smaller areas like "halves" and "quarters." Legal descriptions based on this system identify the precise location of a particular property on this massive grid.

Here is an example of a rectangular survey system legal description: *The northeast quarter of section 27, township 18 south, range 5 west, Willamette Meridian, Standard Baseline.*

- Lot and Block System:

  This system is used in most urban and suburban communities. A raw tract of land is surveyed and broken up into smaller numbered blocks and the blocks are further broken down into individually numbered lots. The map that shows this breakdown—called a "Plat Map"—is filed with the County Register of Deeds for permanent reference. When conveying property within the subdivision, the legal description refers to the subdivision or plat, the corresponding lot number within that plat map, and some reference to plat book number and page number where the original plat map is recorded.

  An example of a lot and block legal description is as follows: *Lot 212 on the plat of Monte Carlo, Block 7, of record in Plat Book 37, Page 96, County Register of Deeds Office.*

At the tax sale auction

When you go to the actual tax sale auction, use the same auction strategies we discussed in Chapter 7. Determine your maximum bid on each property before you even show up at the auction and make sure that you can easily identify any property going on the block solely by its legal description. Believe me, you'll be more than embarrassed if you accidentally buy the wrong property.

Finally, make sure that you completely understand the bidding process for tax sales in your state. Not every state has you simply bid up the price of the tax deed or tax lien certificate. In Michigan, for example, when two or more investors are interested in the same property, they don't bid up the price. Instead, Michigan is set up so that potential investors bid down the percentage of their ownership in the property. This means that if the property is not redeemed, the winning bidder will not own the property free and clear. He will own a percentage of the property with the delinquent taxpayer owning the remaining percentage. For example, if the winning investor wins by bidding his interest in the property down to 85 percent, that means that if he is not redeemed, he will own 85 percent of the property and the former homeowner will own the other 15 percent. I'm sure you can see what kind of difficulties a situation like that can create. If you're not completely clear on the bidding process, keep asking questions until it becomes clear.

Summary

Putting your money into delinquent property tax instruments can be among the most lucrative—and safest—investments you'll ever find. Many counties go out of their way to help those who generate revenue for the county by investing in tax deeds or liens. Always do your homework before bidding on a property, and whenever possible, check out the inside of the property. Make sure that you completely understand the bidding process for tax sales in your state, or you can get yourself embroiled in difficult and costly situations.

CHAPTER 11

How and Where to Find No-Money-Down Deals

It wouldn't surprise me at all if this were the first chapter you've turned to after picking up this book. The dream of making a ton of money without having to put up any of your own is what convinces many would-be real estate investors to see what this business is all about. The late-night-TV real estate gurus certainly do make it seem as if there are no-money-down deals around every corner just waiting to be harvested. (And for just $295.95, they will tell you everything you need to know to get started today.) So your question is, "Are there really no-money-down deals out there that would allow me to make a big profit?" The answer to your question is a resounding, "Yes, there really are no-money-down deals that can earn a big profit for you." But before we talk about finding those deals, let's take a look at what "no money down" means.

What is a no-money-down deal?

In a no-money-down deal, you're basically looking to control a piece of property without any money coming out of your pocket.

That control will require the cooperation of a properly motivated seller who is willing to finance your purchase, hold a second mortgage in lieu of a down payment, or provide you with an option to purchase the property at a later date. Then, once you've secured his or her cooperation, you can go out and find your own buyer or seller. The idea is to control the property for a short time before flipping it to another buyer and collecting the spread between what you paid for it and what you sold it for.

Finding no-money-down deals

As I told you earlier, there are plenty of no-money-down deals out there just waiting to be snatched up. But this comes with a caveat. No-money-down deals are much more difficult to find if you spend all of your time just looking for that type of real estate investment. I realize that this may sound a little peculiar, but think of it this way: No-money-down deals are like love—they're extremely difficult to find if you're looking for them, yet they have a way of falling right into your lap as soon as your attention is diverted. What this means is that you should learn what a potential no-money-down deal looks like and how to put it together, but at the same time, you should be chasing down other types of deals, like foreclosure and tax sale properties, and cash acquisitions of distressed houses. Then, when a no-money-down deal presents itself, you can grab it.

Cast a wide net

In addition to the fact that you are more likely to come across profitable no-money-down transactions while you're in the process of seeking out other types of real estate investments, if your focus is solely on no-money-down transactions, you will almost certainly be forced to walk away from prime deals that you come across because you have no access to cash. So, keep a list of prospective investors handy; that way, you'll be prepared for deals that require a cash investment, as well as no-money-down transactions. An additional advantage is that you will be establishing relationships with your moneypeople.

Prospecting for no-money-down deals

The most important ingredient for putting together a no-money-down deal is a motivated seller. You want to identify a homeowner who—for real or imagined reasons—*HAS* to sell his or her home, someone who feels the pressure to get the deal done quickly. Another important element is that the seller has to be in the financial position to participate in a no-money-down transaction. If he or she needs immediate cash out of the sale, that could be a problem for you, although there are ways around that, as I'll show you a little bit later. From a financial perspective, the best prospect for a zero-cash deal is someone who owns his or her home free and clear.

How and where to find prospects

There are lots of ways to beat prospects out of the bushes. You just have to invest some time and effort. Sources for prospective no-money-down sellers include

- For Sale By Owners. They are selling on their own either because they don't want to pay a real estate commission or because they think they can do a better job than a Realtor. Either way, their frugality and/or self-confidence may make them willing to listen to out-of-the-box thinking. They've already proven that they're not afraid of going against the grain.
- Current landlords who are looking to exit the rental business. Who knows the importance of cash flow better than someone with firsthand experience? Another benefit of buying from your peers is that they are more likely to view the transaction as an unemotional business decision than a homeowner who has lived in the house for any length of time.

- Homeowners with "For Sale" or "For Rent" ads in the newspaper classifieds. Their intentions are pretty clear, but if they've been running into any trouble finding buyers or tenants, they may be willing to listen to creative ideas.
- People whose jobs have been transferred out of town. You can find these motivated sellers by networking with the relocation departments of any large companies in your area.
- Retirees who are looking to move or downsize their home. This group is the most likely to own a property free and clear, an important distinction, as you'll find out later in the chapter. Additionally, they are the group who are usually hit the hardest by the tax consequences of the large lump-sum capital gain a home sale could bring.
- Prospects who respond to your own classified ads. Desperate sellers will respond to any lead they believe might give them a chance to unload their home. Your ad could read something like: "Trying to sell or rent your property? Let us end your landlord headaches. We buy and lease-option properties on a long-term basis. We put together deals on the most difficult-to-sell properties in the marketplace. Your property not selling? Let us come up with a creative plan that will get the job done!"

Structuring the no-money-down deal

Once you find a motivated buyer, what should you do? Well, that all depends upon which approach you want to take and the unique situation of the homeowner. The following are some of the most effective techniques for putting together no-money-down deals.

Lease-Options

A lease-option provides you with a rental lease of the subject property, and the option to purchase the property by some later date at a predetermined price. There are a few ways you can use the lease-option to make money. The least complicated is to sign the lease, move into the property, and buy the property before the option expires. From an investment standpoint, this approach really only makes sense if you are purchasing a multiunit building such as a duplex or triplex, or if you intend to move into the house, fix it up, and then make money by either selling or renting it as you upgrade to your next home.

Another way to profit from a lease-option is to create a spread for yourself by becoming the middleman in a pair of transactions. In the first one, you negotiate a lease-option with the homeowner. Then, in the second deal, you turn around and negotiate another lease-option on the same property with a buyer. For example, let's say that a motivated seller has his or her home listed FSBO for $100,000. You negotiate a two-year lease at $850 a month, with an option to purchase the house at $92,000 anytime before the end of the lease. Then you go out and find a tenant who wants to eventually own a home and sell him or her a two-year lease-option on the same property for $1,100 per month, with a $100 monthly credit toward the purchase price of $100,000. Then, instead of collecting a security deposit, you convince your tenant-buyer to pay a nonrefundable option fee of $1,500 that will be applied to the purchase price if he or she exercises his or her option and buys the house.

What did you just do? You collected $1,500 in cash from your tenant-buyer, and you'll receive $250 cash flow every month. Then, if your tenant-buyer takes the full length of the lease before exercising his or her option, you will receive an additional $4,100 at the closing. That $4,100 comes from your tenant-buyer's purchase price of $100,000, minus your buyer's option fee of $1,500, minus the $2,400 in rent credits he or she earned during the lease, minus your purchase price of $92,000. That makes a grand total of $11,600 ($1,500 option fee + $250 a month for 24 months + $4,100 at closing) put in your pocket over the course of the deal. And what if the tenant walks away without buying the house? Or even without fulfilling the lease? Then you've made $250 a month plus the $1,500 option fee, just for putting the deal together. Now you can choose whether to purchase the home at $92,000, walk away with the money you've already earned, or find another renter to finish out your lease.

The fact that you don't actually have title to the property during the two-year lease has positive and negative attributes. On the plus side, you don't have to pay any taxes or insurance since you don't own anything. Negatively, if anything should happen to the house—fire, flood, etc.—you won't be in a position to collect anything for your interests. Another problem is that because the original owner still holds title to the property, he or she can cloud the title without your knowing it, by taking out a lien on the property or failing to pay property taxes. Also, if you choose your tenant-buyers poorly, they could easily do serious damage (much more than the $1,500 option fee you collect from them) to the home and then disappear, leaving you holding the bag.

Of course, the biggest question about lease-options should be, "Why the heck would a homeowner agree to such a deal in the first place?" The answer is that you have to convince a seller that this is an appealing arrangement. If a seller is not sufficiently motivated to get rid of his house, a lease-option can be an extremely tough sell. Even if he is highly motivated, it's still not easy, but you can change his perspective by explaining the tax benefits of owning a rental property for a couple of years, which would keep him from capital gains taxes on any lump sum he would pull out of the house. You might also tell him that the depreciation of the house might also allow him to offset some of his actual income. If the homeowner needs the money he would get from a sale to cover the down payment of his next property, suggest that he take out a home equity loan on the rental property to cover his next purchase. In addition, the monthly rent you pay him may be sufficient to cover his monthly mortgage payments on a new property, and possibly even offer him some positive cash flow.

Lease-options are a hard sell and difficult to put together, but you can see the profit potential they present. And they remain a good way to get into the real estate investing game when you don't have much money.

Seller financing

Some sellers may be willing to finance your purchase themselves. Basically, this means that instead of your getting a mortgage note with a financial institution, the seller acts as the bank. An agreement similar to a mortgage (depending on your area, it may be called a land contract, deed for trust, or simply seller financing) is drawn up that calls for the buyer to make monthly payments to the former owners of the property. Interest, contract length, and amortization are all figured the same way as in a mortgage. From the buyer's standpoint, it is really no different from traditional financing. From the seller's viewpoint, he is forgoing a lump sum payoff in exchange for regular income. This has some of the same tax advantages for the seller as the lease-option we discussed earlier.

Because this is a transfer of title, the former owner can't really cause you problems by putting additional liens on the house without your knowledge, providing that you record your land contract at the county Register of Deeds office. Unfortunately, recording the land contract can cause other problems if the former owner didn't own the property free and clear. A homeowner who is still paying off an existing mortgage cannot sell his or her home through seller financing without permission if the existing mortgage has a "Due on Sale" clause. This means the entire outstanding balance on that original note becomes due and payable as soon as the property is sold. Unfortunately for you, almost every non-government mortgage written today contains one of these clauses. So although you would be protecting yourself when you record your land contract, you could also be killing the deal, because once the bank activates the Due on Sale clause, someone will have to come up with the cash required to pay off the remaining balance. Seller financing is a bad idea in a case like this, if the seller is unwilling or unable to pay off the balance of any liens.

No matter how much you want a certain property, don't ever consider trying to sneak a seller-financed deal through without the bank's knowing; otherwise, you could be putting yourself in great financial peril. Sooner or later you will have to record your land contract, and the bank will find out. At that point, the bank will be looking for its money. Another danger you face by not recording your land contract in an effort to keep the bank in the dark is that you could be dealing with an unscrupulous seller who, knowing that you didn't record your land contract, may load up the property with liens and mortgages.

Even if you can escape the Due on Sale trap, there's still the not-so-small matter of persuading a seller to enter into this agreement with you with no down payment. If you have a good credit history, you may be able to satisfy the seller with copies of your credit report and solid character references. If your credit isn't stellar, the task becomes more difficult. If the sellers have been trying to sell for some time with little success, offering a premium above and beyond the purchase price could be enough to convince them to take a chance on you. For example, if they are willing to sell the house for $100,000, you could offer to pay $110,000 in exchange for them providing no-money-down seller financing. You could also consider raising the interest rate so they get a better return on their money.

Seller-carried second mortgage

Another approach to buying a property with no money down is to get bank or seller financing for all but the down payment, and then persuade the sellers to carry a short-term mortgage note for the difference, the latter being the seller-carried second mortgage. For instance, let's say you come across a motivated buyer who agrees to sell you his home for $80,000. When you go for financing, the bank requires you to put down 20 percent, or $16,000 (20 percent because you're buying it as an investment property). You ask the seller to accept a five-year mortgage note from you for the $16,000.

It is much easier to get the seller to agree to this kind of arrangement than to the land contract or lease-option deals, because if a seller has more than 20 percent equity in his home, he will receive cash at the closing, and in addition to the cash up front, he will also get five years' worth of regular monthly income.

The biggest hurdle you'll need to overcome with this kind of transaction is the fact that most mortgage lenders won't do the deal if they know that you're not actually putting up any money in the transaction. There are a few ways around this. One way to show the down payment is coming from you is to have friends or family provide you with a gift of the $16,000. Or, you could "sell" some personal property, such as a car, computer, or furniture, for the $16,000 with the verbal agreement that you will buy it right back after the transaction is completed. Once the $16,000 is deposited in your checking account, you can write a check for that amount and turn it in at the closing. Then once the seller-carried second mortgage is signed by everyone, you can close on it and get the $16,000, which you can then use to buy back any personal property or gift money back to people who had given that amount to you previously.

The other way to keep from putting money down through a seller-carried second mortgage is to seek out sellers who have assumable mortgages—notes that don't contain Due on Sale clauses. As I mentioned previously, it's quite rare to find a conventional loan that is assumable. Government loans, however, are all assumable. Buyers looking to take over a VA or FHA loan can do so rather easily. They must pass a credit check mandated by the government and pay for title transfer, recording, and other closing costs. If you assume an FHA loan, you will most likely be required to use the property you purchase as your primary residence. Your goal is to assume the loan and have the seller carry a mortgage note for the balance of the sale price. You can get the property with little or no cash of your own.

Line of credit

It is easier to do deals without any money coming out of your pocket when you can find properties that are significantly undervalued. If the seller is especially motivated and/or the house needs extensive repairs and renovations, you may be able to acquire properties for as little as 40 or 50 percent of its market value when in top shape—although 60 to 80 percent buys are more plentiful. The key to these deals is to be ready to jump on them when they come along. You can be sure that if you hesitate, another investor will swoop in and steal the property from you.

Once you find the property, you can pay for it with a line of credit, such as a small business loan, or even your credit cards if the property is an exceptional deal. You could secure your line against your personal property or other real estate. The interest rate on this money isn't really important because, as you will see, you will be flipping it into another loan rather quickly. The idea is to use your credit line to acquire the property at least 70 to 80 percent below market value and to pay for necessary repairs and renovations. Then, while the repairs are underway, you can start the process of refinancing the house into a regular mortgage note. When financing an investment property, the bank will likely require that 20 to 30 percent equity be left in the house when the mortgage note is signed. If you've done your homework properly and handled the repairs within your budget, you should be able to close the new mortgage and pay off the line of credit funds without any money coming out of your own pocket. In the best deals, it's even possible to walk away from the closing with a check made out to you. If you buy a house for $45,000 on a line of credit and then put $15,000 into it for repairs, you are into it for $60,000. If that house is worth $100,000 when fixed up and you get an 80 percent mortgage on it, that means in addition to paying all your bills, you will walk away from the mortgage closing with $20,000 in your pocket.

The other source of funding that you can tap for a highly undervalued property is hard money, which is high-interest funds that lenders provide to investors for real estate deals. A hard money loan is typically a short-term note that's designed to allow the investor to get the funds necessary to handle repairs and renovations. Because this kind of loan will probably be paid back in a year or less, borrowers are more willing to pay upfront fees and higher interest rates. Hard money lending was discussed more thoroughly in Chapter 4.

This approach to investing in real estate also works with friends, family, acquaintances, and other investors who are willing to provide you with capital. Use their funds to acquire and repair the property and then refinance it into a normal mortgage, the equity you've created in the house canceling out the need to put up a down payment.

VA mortgages

If you are a veteran, the Veteran's Administration will provide you with a no-money-down loan on a house. The only stipulations are that the property can contain no more than four units and you have to live in one of the units after the deal is closed. Call the VA office nearest you for details on the programs they provide.

What it takes to succeed in no-money-down deals

To be successful and make a profit in no-money-down transactions, you obviously don't need money. What you'll need, instead, is patience and persistence. Every time you feel like quitting, you'll have to keep at it a little bit longer. You will eventually find the deals if you just stick with it. Having some sales and negotiating skills will be helpful as well. Chances are that prospective sellers will need some serious convincing before they agree to do your deal. With you having no financial stake in the property, the owners will quite naturally believe that they are taking on all of the risk in the transaction. Knowing how to present the deal in a manner that points out the benefits to the sellers will be hugely important if you want them to agree to close the transaction.

As you seek out no-money-down deals, don't become obsessed with them to the point where you start believing that a deal is good simply because you don't have to put up any money. Carefully analyze what the future cost will be and what kind of a profit you are likely to make on the property.

Know when to call in the experts

I strongly recommend that you consult with a real estate attorney when putting any of the practices I discuss in this chapter (and throughout the book, for that matter!) into action. As I've said several times, real estate laws vary widely from state to state. What might be perfectly legal in one area could be illegal in another. Another benefit of hiring a lawyer is that he or she will help you draw up documents, paperwork, and contracts that will protect you in case a transaction goes sour. If you don't seek out legal counsel, you are operating entirely at your own risk—and that risk could cost you the price of a house or more. Is it really worth that kind of exposure to save a few bucks? At the least, have an attorney help you put together some fill-in-the-blank contracts for each type of no-money-down deal you plan on doing.

Other experts you would do well to hire are a professional appraiser and a home inspector. You should do the same careful research in these areas as you would if you were putting your own money into the transaction, and the insights of these experts are a valuable tool that will be worth the investment.

Summary

There really are no-money-down deals that can earn a big profit for you, but they are much more difficult to find if you spend all of your time just looking for that type of real estate investment. Sources for prospective no-money-down sellers include FSBOs, current landlords trying to sell, and retirees looking to downsize, to name a few. Once you find a motivated buyer, some of the most effective techniques for putting together no-money-down transactions include lease-options, seller-carried second mortgages, and seller financing. And in order to succeed in no-money-down deals, what you'll need instead of cash is patience and persistence. Finally, at the risk of repeating myself, leave the legal work to the experts.

CHAPTER 12

Finding Deals at Auctions

We briefly covered some types of auctions in Chapters 7 and 10. Bank foreclosures, tax sales, and other distressed property sales are what most Americans picture when thinking about real estate auctions. In reality, many different kinds of real estate are moved at many different kinds of auctions across the country.

There certainly are many distressed property sales, but you can also find auctions of raw and subdivided land, commercial buildings, unsold condominium units, and single-family homes in outstanding condition. These properties may be sold, one or two per auction, right on the front porch of the subject house, a hundred per auction in a hotel ballroom, or even on the web during an Internet auction. Don't allow yourself to have preconceived notions about how a real estate auction should look or what will be available at one. Keeping an open mind at an auction sale will bring many more opportunities to profit.

I've been fascinated by auctions ever since I visited Australia a few years ago on a speaking tour. Like many investors in America, I was stuck in the mindset that real estate auctions are mainly for distressed properties. Imagine my surprise when I learned that real estate in Australia is generally sold at auction. Instead of listing them on a Multiple Listing Service and waiting for buyers to make offers as we do here, the Australians put the home on the auction block and unearth a buyer. It doesn't matter if your house is worth $50,000 or $5 million. It's just the way things are done there.

You don't see many auctions in Michigan like those in Australia, but the trip did teach me to keep my eyes—and mind—open to out-of-the-ordinary ways to buy and sell real estate. That's why I was ready to embrace the Internet real estate auction concept when it was presented in Detroit not too long ago. I got so excited bidding on properties and watching the press it generated in Southeastern Michigan that within few days of its arrival, I was on the phone with the auction company trying to meet them and get them to team up with me on another auction here in Detroit.

That's how I met my friend Mike Keracher. He is a 15-year veteran of the live auction business and currently is one of the owners and founders of AMSauctions.com, an online auction company that sells mainly bank- and investor-owned property. AMS is the leader in online real estate sales with more than 1,000 bank-owned houses sold through totally online auctions since June 2000.

Getting started

"The most effective notice of upcoming sales is sent out by direct mail," Mike says. "Watch the real estate section of your newspaper for auction listings and advertisements. Then, when you go to the sales, get your name on the mailing list. Once you do this a few times, you'll get notice by mail of most sales going on in your area."

The next place to go, according to Mike, is to developers and builders. "Some of the best auctions I've seen are developer close-outs," he says. Developers like to get in and out of projects as quickly as possible. It drives them nuts being forced to wait for a few odd lots and spec houses to sell before they can free up their cash to get a new project underway.

"Let's say a developer is wrapping up a project with 100 or more home sites," Mike explains. "All that are left are 10 to 15 lots and maybe a few spec houses. The developer wants to be rid of the left-overs, but he doesn't want to just give them away. So he auctions them off and moves on to the next project." He adds, "Condominium projects often have the same kinds of deals. The bank wants the loan paid off, so the builder auctions off the last few remaining unsold units."

Ballroom auctions

Mike got his start putting together huge events in cities with anywhere from 25 to 200 properties auctioned off in a single day in an auditorium or hotel ballroom. These auctions almost exclusively sold bank-owned properties. As Mike explains, "In the secondary mortgage market, banks buy huge packages of loans in blocks of 1,000 to 2,000 at a time. Eighty percent of these loans are good while 20 percent are bad and end up in foreclosure." So in the case of a 2,000-loan package, the bank would end up foreclosing on 400 properties. Some of these would be sold to investors at the foreclosure auction, leaving the bank with 350 or more homes on its real estate owned (REO) list for each loan package purchased. These properties eat up time and resources while the bank owns them.

Mike's ballroom auctions provided the banks with an outlet to sell the REO properties directly to investors so they could liquidate many of the homes and get at least a marginal return on these assets. "REOs are a great market for investors because the supplier of the product has no personal value attached to the house or the sale," Mike says. "They can make pure business decisions without emotions getting in the way."

Internet auctions

Mike's company, AMS Auctions, has taken the ballroom auction concept to the Internet. You can see how it all works—and whether or not properties are offered for sale in your area—by visiting the website at www.amsauctions.com.

The auction is set up similar to the popular web auction site eBay. Most listings contain a photo, brief property description, and the contact information of a local real estate agent who can show the house in person. When they decide to bid, buyers register at the site with a valid credit card, which provides AMS with proof the bidder is an adult. The credit card is never charged unless the winning bidder refuses to close the deal. It's been a pretty good system: Only about 1 percent of successful bidders has failed to close since AMS has been operating online. The normal fallout rate for ballroom auctions is 3 to 4 percent. Each property has a reserve price below which the bank will not sell it, but the bidding system lets you know when the reserve has been met.

The main difference between the virtual and real-world auctions is that the online version is on the block for two weeks rather than just for one night. According to Mike, this helps bidders make better-informed decisions. "Mom and Pop bidders are often intimidated at the ballroom auctions," he says. "They don't want to be forced to make a snap decision. I've seen people who show up wanting a specific property and leave without bidding on it because they are afraid they'll make a mistake. The Internet takes away the fear factor. They have 14 days to make a decision. If someone raises the bid, they can go back and look at the house as many times as they like until they're comfortable enough to raise their own bid. Plus, bidders can do this on their own schedule. They like the fact that they can bid on properties from the comfort of their own home at any time of the day."

Auction tips

Here are some general rules that will serve you well at just about any kind of auction:

- *Don't Forget about the Buyer Premium* In traditional American real estate transactions, the seller pays a commission to both the listing and selling agents that comes out of the proceeds of the sale. At an auction, the commission is not included in the proceeds. It is added on top of the sale price in the form of a buyer premium. For example, if you spend $100,000 and the buyer premium is 5 percent, your purchase will actually cost you $105,000.

- *Figure Out Your Maximum Purchase Price and Don't Bid Over It* I've mentioned this rule in previous chapters, but it's worth repeating here. If you properly do your homework before the auction, there's no good reason to make a rash decision during the heat of the bidding. If you can't control yourself at the auction, avoid doing something that you'll regret later. Figure out your maximum bid and send someone else to bid in your place.
- *An Investor Can't Beat a Homeowner* There will be times when you realize the person you're bidding against is trying to purchase the property for his personal residence or it's the guy who lives next door who wants to double the size of his lot. Continue to follow your bidding strategy, but realize you probably won't get the house. These kinds of bidders are willing to spend more money than an investor, because they are emotionally involved in the process. Let them have the house and set your sights on something else.
- *Don't Get Your Heart Set on One Particular Property* At ballroom auctions, many investors make the mistake of choosing the property they want the most, letting good ones get away while they wait for the best one to go on the block. Often, others are also waiting for the same property, and you wind up missing out on good buys without even getting the one for which you waited. Choose several properties you'd like, bid on them as they come up, and be satisfied with whatever you get.
- *Deals Are Lurking Late in the Auction* Money is not endless. The big purchasers at a ballroom auction often spend all of their money and get out the door as early as possible. It's in the final hour of the auction—when everyone else has spent

their money and left—that you can often find great buys because the competition has disappeared.

- *Absolute Auctions Don't Usually Offer Any Advantage to Investors* Most auctions are reserve auctions in which the buyer has a minimum price at which he's willing to sell the property. Of course the bidders don't know what that price is. When the auction is absolute, however, it means the property is going to be sold that day even if only one person makes a bid. When investors see an absolute auction advertised, they get excited and dream of buying a $100,000 property for $200. The problem is that word "absolute" draws similar investors out of the woodwork, and many times the purchase price ends up being higher than what that same property would draw at a reserve auction. Of course, if you go to enough auctions and meet enough investors, you'll hear true stories about people who bought great properties for ridiculously low prices at absolute auctions. The common thread in all of these stories is that the turnout at the auction was unusually low for some reason, such as a snowstorm, huge highway accident or some other random event. So, if you want to chase the great white whale of an absolute auction steal, you may want to get a four-wheel-drive vehicle with good snow tires.

Selling your own property at auction

I believe listing and selling property through normal channels is still the best way to go, but auctions can offer some advantages you don't get with an MLS listing. For instance, it offers you the opportunity to know your property will be sold on a given day, if you're willing to go absolute or are confident that there is a good chance it will be sold that day if you maintain a reserve price. If you've decided to take the auction route to selling your property, here are some tips to help you be more successful.

- *Hire a Reputable Auctioneer* Check his credentials with the National Auctioneers Association, the Better Business Bureau, and your local board of Realtors. It will help your sale if the auction company offers a guaranteed financing program to purchasers at the auction.
- *Let Your Property Decide If It Will Be Sold in a Standalone Auction or Part of a Ballroom Sale* If you have an inexpensive house that would be attractive to investors, it would probably sell for more money if it's included in a pool of similar houses, sold to a roomful of investors. If the house is a one-of-a-kind showplace, you'll do much better if it's the featured act.
- *You Need Marketing* You want your auction company to provide a full marketing and advertising campaign, including direct mail, ads in your local paper's real estate section, and signs in the front yard. Unless you agree to sell your property in an absolute auction, expect to pay for most of the marketing expenses yourself.
- *Provide Access to the Property* Encourage your auction company to hold and staff open houses before the sale takes place. Get a lockbox on the door so potential buyers can visit the property in the weeks leading up to the auction.
- *Have Important Paperwork Available for Inspection* Get an appraisal in advance, especially if your reserve is less than market value. Provide potential buyers with a home inspector's report prior to the sale, since by law you have to reveal any known defects anyway. Items such as these raise buyer confidence in the property, which will ultimately raise the purchase price.

CHAPTER 13

Property Acquisition Checklists, Forms, and Letters

When the time comes to try and put all of the different acquisition methods to work, it can become somewhat confusing and quite easy to forget important aspects of the process. That's the purpose of this chapter—to help you keep all of your ducks in a row while running down deals. What follows is an outline of the property acquisition process along with some forms and sample letters that will make your work easier and more productive.

Marketing Checklist: Identify Prospective Properties

Find advertised properties through

- ❑ Foreclosure listings
- ❑ For Sale By Owner classified ads and yard signs
- ❑ MLS listings
- ❑ HUD and VA foreclosures
- ❑ Tax sales

Locate prospects through marketing and networking

- ❑ Place classified advertisements for
  - Cash buys
  - Foreclosures
- ❑ Place flyers at supermarkets, community centers (bulletin boards), restaurants, your doctor's office, and anywhere else you go.
- ❑ Send direct mail to
  - Homeowners, addressing their particular situation, such as
    - ✓ For sale by owners
    - ✓ Foreclosures
    - ✓ Tax sale properties
    - ✓ Prospective paper deals
  - Attorneys who specialize in
    - ✓ Probate
    - ✓ Foreclosure
    - ✓ Divorce
    - ✓ Bankruptcy
    - ✓ General real estate
- ❑ Bank REOs

- ❑ Your real estate advisers, including
  - Realtor
  - Real estate attorney
  - Banker/Mortgage broker
  - Contractors
  - Property managers

Research checklist: Learn about the property

—Off-site research

- ❑ Chain of title
  - Search for:
    - ✓ Mortgages
    - ✓ Unpaid property taxes and special assessments
    - ✓ Mechanic's liens
    - ✓ Fixture filings
    - ✓ IRS and state tax liens
- ❑ Realtor
  - Find MLS comparable sales and listings
  - What is property value appreciation in area over past 2–3 years

—On-site research—get photos and take detailed notes

- ❑ Outside
  - Home itself
    - ✓ Windows
    - ✓ Roof
    - ✓ Brick and/or siding
    - ✓ Gutters
    - ✓ Foundation
    - ✓ Signs of dry rot or termite damage
  - Surrounding property
    - ✓ Landscaping
    - ✓ Pavement

- ✓ Porch
- ✓ Decks
- ✓ Garage
- ✓ Fences
- ✓ Debris

❑ Inside

- General
  - ✓ Carpet
  - ✓ Paint and wallpaper
  - ✓ Linoleum
  - ✓ Electrical
  - ✓ Plumbing
  - ✓ Heating and cooling units
  - ✓ Signs of past damage from water, fire, etc.
- Kitchen and Bathroom
  - ✓ Plumbing fixtures and water pressure
  - ✓ Cupboards
  - ✓ Tile
  - ✓ Appliances

❑ Interview owners

- History
  - ✓ Length of residence
  - ✓ Kids
  - ✓ Pets
  - ✓ Fire, flood, tornado, earthquake damage
  - ✓ Recent renovations
  - ✓ Any problems with major systems
  - ✓ Age of roof, furnace, heating and cooling, etc.
- Plans and opinions
  - ✓ Date they can be out of house
  - ✓ What they believe the value of the house to be
  - ✓ Amount of money they hope to get for the house

- ✓ Earliest and latest possible closing dates
- ✓ Fixtures and appliances that will be left behind
- ✓ Fixtures and appliances that will be removed
- ✓ Repairs/renovations that currently need to be done
- ✓ Other investors they have spoken to

Pricing checklist: Figure out what the property is worth and what you'll pay for it

- Determine market value
  - ❑ Get professional help from your advisers
    - Realtor—MLS comparable sales
    - Licensed appraiser
    - Home inspector
  - ❑ Potential monthly rent
- Plans for property
  - ❑ Hold long term
    - Lease to tenant
  - ❑ Hold for a few years
    - Move in, renovate, sell, and move out
  - ❑ Hold short term
    - Repair and flip
- Determine purchase price
  - ❑ Start with acquisition/repair expenses
    - Paint and carpet
    - Repairs and renovations
    - Unexpected expenses—the older the home, the more money should be allotted for this area
    - Back taxes and special assessments
    - Mortgage and lien payoffs
    - Real estate commissions
    - Interest on borrowed funds

- Closing costs
- Recording fees
- Insurance

❑ Flipper property—Determine acceptable purchase price by subtracting profit spread and acquisition/repair expenses from market value of completed home

❑ Rental property—Determine acceptable purchase price based on cash flow property will produce

- Research probable monthly rent property will generate
- Figure out what long-term monthly cash outflow will be required to cover acquisition/repair expenses and rental expenses, including
  - ✓ Principal and interest payment
  - ✓ Property taxes
  - ✓ Insurance
  - ✓ Maintenance
  - ✓ Utilities and services supplied to tenant

Purchasing checklist: Steps to take in completing a purchase

- Write purchase offer
  - ❑ Get professional help from attorney or Realtor
  - ❑ Make it contingent upon a full appraisal of the home
  - ❑ Complete title search and/or title insurance
  - ❑ Consider hiring a professional closing coordinator to close the transaction
- Auction purchases
  - ❑ Do your homework before the auction
    - Visit an auction before bidding on a property to learn
      - ✓ Terms of sale
      - ✓ Length of redemption period, if any
      - ✓ Bidding styles of your potential competition

- Attempt to get into the house before the sale—if you can't, figure that into your pricing:
  - ✓ The outside look of the property will give you clues to the inside condition
  - ✓ Always figure on new paint and carpet throughout the house
  - ✓ The older the property, the more funds you'll have to set aside for "unexpected" expenses
  - ✓ Talk to the neighbors
- Double and triple check to make sure you know exactly what position you are buying at the sale (don't buy a second lien when you want a first!)
- Know maximum bid before arriving

❑ Stay cool at the auction

- Don't get drawn into bidding wars—stick to your predetermined maximum bid

❑ After the auction

- Approach the bank or tax sale representative about buying the property if it didn't sell to an investor
- Notify your Realtor of the property address so he or she can watch for it when it is listed on the MLS

Acquisition checklist: After the deal is made

- Immediately get insurance
- Taking possession
  - ❑ Discuss redemption/acquisition laws and regulations with a real estate attorney or knowledgeable county official
  - ❑ If allowed, change locks and take possession
  - ❑ If former owner remains in home past redemption period, start eviction process
    - Drop off letter asking former owner to discuss his or her intentions with you
    - Hire attorney to begin eviction procedure

PROPERTY EVALUATION FORM #1
OFFSITE RESEARCH

Type of Acquisition:

- ❑ Cash Acquisition—No Realtor
- ❑ MLS Listing—Thru Realtor
- ❑ Foreclosure
- ❑ Mortgage Note Purchase
- ❑ Tax Sale
- ❑ Bank REO
- ❑ HUD / VA Foreclosure

Location & Legal Information:

Property Address: ______________________________

City: ______________________ ZIP Code: ______________________

Legal Description: ______________________________

County: ______________________ Tax ID #: ______________________

Homeowner Name: ______________________________

Mailing Address: ______________________________

City: ______________ State: __________ ZIP: __________

Home Phone: ______________________ Work Phone: ______________________

Transfer Details:

Did homeowner take title to property through a warranty deed? ______________

If no, what kind of deed was it? ______________________________

Deed Date: ______________________ Original Purchase Price: ______________

Liens on Title:

1st Position Lien Holder: ______________________________

Contact Person: ______________________ Amount of Lien: ______________

Date of Lien: ______________________ Book & Page Recorded: ______________

Address: ______________________________

City: ______________________ State: ________ ZIP: __________

Phone: ______________________ Fax: ______________________

2nd Position Lien Holder: ______________________________

Contact Person: ______________ Amount of Lien: ______________

Date of Lien: ______________ Book & Page Recorded: __________

Address: ______________________________

City: ______________ State: ______ ZIP: __________

Phone: ______________ Fax: ______________

3rd Position Lien Holder: ______________________________

Contact Person: ______________ Amount of Lien: ______________

Date of Lien: ______________ Book & Page Recorded: __________

Address: ______________________________

City: ______________ State: ______ ZIP: __________

Phone: ______________ Fax: ______________

Other Lien Holders: ______________________________

____

____

Other Items on Title:

Back Property Taxes: ______________________________

Special Tax Assessments: ______________________________

Fixture Filings: ______________________________

Judgments: ______________________________

Bankruptcies: ______________________________

Powers of Attorney: ______________________________

Divorce Decrees: ______________________________

Death Notices: ______________________________

QuitClaim Deeds: ______________________________

Legal Name Changes: ______________________________

Affidavits: ______________________________

If Foreclosure Property:

Insertion Dates: ______________________________

Sale Date: ______________ Sale Time: ______________

Lien Position: ______________________________

Loan Amount: ______________ Interest Rate: ______________

Attorney / Substitute Trustee: ______________________

Firm: ______________ Contact Person: ______________

Address: ______________________________

City: ______________ State: ______ ZIP: __________

Phone: ______________ Fax: ______________

Redemption Date: ______________________________

Last Day to Redeem: ______________________________

Does this foreclosure have good potential to be a Paper Deal? ___**YES** ___**NO**

If Tax Sale Property:

Sale Date: ______________ Sale Time: ______________

Tax Year(s) Being Sold: ______________________________

Other Tax Years Outstanding: ______________________

Person conducting Tax Sale: ______________________

Title: ______________ Firm / Dept.: ______________

Address: ______________________________

City: ______________ State: ______ ZIP: __________

Phone: ______________ Fax: ______________

Redemption Date: ______________________________

Last Day to Redeem: ______________________________

Property Evaluation Form #2
Outside the Property

Property Address: ____________________

Neighborhood Details:

Neighborhood is predominantly:

❑ Brick ❑ Frame ❑ Mix

Neighborhood Rating:

❑ Poor ❑ Fair ❑ Good ❑ Excellent

Listings in the Neighborhood:

Address: ________ Phone: ________ Asking Price: ________

Address: ________ Phone: ________ Asking Price: ________

Address: ________ Phone: ________ Asking Price: ________

Property Tenancy:

Property is: ❑ Vacant ❑ Owner Occupied ❑ Tenant Occupied

Tenant Info: How long in home? ________ Monthly Rent: ________

House Details:

Yr Built: ________ Sq Footage: ________ Lot Size: ________

Garage—Size: ____________________

Condition: ❑ Poor ❑ Fair ❑ Good

Driveway Type: ____________________

Condition: ❑ Poor ❑ Fair ❑ Good

Roof Type: ________ Estimated Age: ________

Condition: ❑ Poor ❑ Fair ❑ Good

Type of Construction:

❑ Brick ❑ Frame ❑ Block

❑ Aluminum ❑ Asbestos ❑ Vinyl

Condition: ❑ Poor ❑ Fair ❑ Good

House Style:

❑ Tudor	❑ Bungalow	❑ Ranch	❑ Split-Level
❑ Colonial	❑ Cape Cod	❑ Multi-Family	❑ Other

Foundation:

❑ Basement	❑ Slab	❑ Crawl	❑ Piers

Storm Doors / Storm Windows / Screens:

Condition:	❑ Poor	❑ Fair	❑ Good

Windows:

❑ Vinyl	❑ Aluminum	❑ Wood	❑ Other
Condition:	❑ Poor	❑ Fair	❑ Good

Fence:	❑ Chain	❑ Wood	❑ Wire
Condition:	❑ Poor	❑ Fair	❑ Good

Landscaping:

Condition:	❑ Poor	❑ Fair	❑ Good

Porch:	❑ Cement	❑ Wood	❑ Brick
Condition:	❑ Poor	❑ Fair	❑ Good

Steps:	❑ Cement	❑ Wood	❑ Brick
Condition:	❑ Poor	❑ Fair	❑ Good

Door:	❑ Wood	❑ Steel	❑ Vinyl
Condition:	❑ Poor	❑ Fair	❑ Good

ADDITIONAL NOTES:

PROPERTY EVALUATION FORM #3
INSIDE THE PROPERTY

Property Address: ______________________________

Occupant reported problems:

❑ Electrical ❑ Plumbing ❑ Heating ❑ Leaks ❑ Other

Details: ______________________________

____

GENERAL CONDITION:

Problems with:

❑ Floor / Carpet ❑ Walls ❑ Ceilings

❑ Electrical ❑ Plumbing ❑ Heating/Cooling Units

Details: ______________________________

____

Overall Condition:

❑ Poor ❑ Fair ❑ Good ❑ Excellent

Special Features: ______________________________

____

____

KITCHEN:

Problems with:

❑ Water Pressure ❑ Floor ❑ Counter Tops

❑ Lights ❑ Cabinets ❑ Sink

Details: ______________________________

____

Overall Condition:

❑ Poor ❑ Fair ❑ Good ❑ Excellent

Kitchen Notes: ______________________________

____

BATHROOMS—Number of Bathrooms in House: ____________

Problems with:

- ❑ Water Pressure
- ❑ Floor
- ❑ Tub / Shower
- ❑ Lights
- ❑ Vanity
- ❑ Sink
- ❑ Tile
- ❑ Mirror

Details: ____

____

Overall Condition:

❑ Poor ❑ Fair ❑ Good ❑ Excellent

Bathroom Notes: ____

____

OTHER ROOMS—Number of Bedrooms: ______________

Room #1 Name: ____

Overall Condition:

❑ Poor ❑ Fair ❑ Good ❑ Excellent

Notes: ____

____

Room #2 Name: ____

Overall Condition:

❑ Poor ❑ Fair ❑ Good ❑ Excellent

Notes: ____

____

Room #3 Name: ____

Overall Condition:

❑ Poor ❑ Fair ❑ Good ❑ Excellent

Notes: ____

____

Room #4 Name: ____

Overall Condition:

❑ Poor ❑ Fair ❑ Good ❑ Excellent

Notes: ____

____

Room #5 Name: ______________________________

Overall Condition:

❑ Poor ❑ Fair ❑ Good ❑ Excellent

Notes: ______________________________

____

Room #6 Name: ______________________________

Overall Condition:

❑ Poor ❑ Fair ❑ Good ❑ Excellent

Notes: ______________________________

____

Room #7 Name: ______________________________

Overall Condition:

❑ Poor ❑ Fair ❑ Good ❑ Excellent

Notes: ______________________________

____

ADDITIONAL NOTES:

____

____

____

____

____

____

____

____

____

____

____

____

PROPERTY EVALUATION FORM #4
DEAL ANALYSIS FORM—FLIPPERS

Property Address: ______________________________

Flipper Evaluation:

Market Value of Completed Home: $______________________________

Required Repairs: ____________________ Cost: $ ________________

____________________ Cost: $ ________________

____________________ Cost: $ ________________

____________________ Cost: $ ________________

____________________ Cost: $ ________________

____________________ Cost: $ ________________

____________________ Cost: $ ________________

Total Anticipated Repair Expenses: $ ________________

Commissions/Closing Costs: ____________ Cost: $ ________________

____________________ Cost: $ ________________

____________________ Cost: $ ________________

____________________ Cost: $ ________________

____________________ Cost: $ ________________

____________________ Cost: $ ________________

Total Anticipated Closing Costs: $ ________________

Carrying Costs (Interest, Insurance, Utilities, etc):

____________________ Cost: $ ________________

____________________ Cost: $ ________________

____________________ Cost: $ ________________

____________________ Cost: $ ________________

____________________ Cost: $ ________________

Total Anticipated Carrying Costs: $ ________________

Spread: $ ________________

TOTAL ANTICIPATED COSTS

(Repairs + Closing + Carrying + Spread) $ ________________

MAXIMUM PURCHASE PRICE

(Improved Property Value - Total Costs): $ ________________

Property Evaluation Form #5
Deal Analysis Form—Rentals

Property Address: ______________________________

Rental Evaluation:

Anticipated Monthly Rental Income: $ ______________________

Anticipated Monthly Rental Expenses (Except Principal & Interest Payment):

Insurance: $ __________

Property Taxes: $ __________

Maintenance: $ __________

Utilities: $ __________

Services Provided to Tenant: $ __________

Miscellaneous Expenses (20% of Monthly Rent): $ __________

Other Expenses: ____________________ $ __________

____________________ $ __________

Total Anticipated Monthly Expenses: $ __________

Break-even Principal & Interest Payment: $ __________

(Monthly Rent – Monthly Expenses): $ __________

If monthly P&I payment is greater than this number, cash flow will be negative.

If monthly P&I payment is less than this number, cash flow will be positive.

Bankruptcy Attorney Letter

This letter can be modified and also sent to attorneys who specialize in probate, foreclosure, and divorce.

Robert Phillips, Attorney-at-Law
321 North Avenue
Anywhere, USA

Dear Mr. Phillips:

My name is Ralph Roberts. I buy and sell real estate in the area, and I'm writing you today for a pair of reasons.

First of all, while checking out cash acquisition leads, I regularly come into contact with people with an interest in gaining information about bankruptcy laws and regulations. And many of them, I believe, would benefit from having access to the legal advice a professional such as you could offer. I would like your permission to refer these prospects to you.

Second, it recently occurred to me that in the course of your work you might come across individuals who would benefit from cashing out of real estate quickly. The next time you identify a client or acquaintance in this position, I would be grateful if you would give me the opportunity to bid on the property. As I mentioned above, I specialize in real estate cash acquisitions and, once a deal is struck, I have the ability to close it in 24 hours or less.

I truly believe that we can create a win-win situation by staying in contact and working together on the types of transactions I've outlined in this letter. Please give me a call at (810) 555-1234 if you have any questions. I look forward to speaking with you soon.

Sincerely,

Ralph Roberts

General Foreclosure Letter

With a few minor adjustments, this letter could also be sent to homeowners facing tax sales.

John and Mary Smith
123 South Avenue
Anywhere, USA

Dear Mr. and Mrs. Smith:

The scheduled Foreclosure Auction of your home is quickly approaching.

Just so that you are completely aware of what's going on here, **I believe that it is *very important* that you *fully* understand what will happen if your house goes on that auction block.** At the Foreclosure Sale, ***your property* will be sold to the highest bidder.** If no investor comes forward to bid on your property, it will be turned over to the bank that holds your mortgage. Either way, ***you will no longer own your home* once the sale takes place.**

If you continue to do nothing, you *will* lose your home. That is a harsh statement, but I want to be perfectly clear so that I know you are completely aware of your situation and the consequences of your actions—or inaction.

If you call me at (810) 555-1234, I can answer any questions you may have about the foreclosure process. I regularly buy and sell properties in this area and I do have some unique insights that may be helpful to you. If selling your home is the answer to your dilemma, I am prepared to make a cash offer. I can close transactions in 24 hours or less, and I will do my best to put some money in your pocket and help you salvage what's left of your credit rating.

Please, at least call me to let me know that you do indeed understand what is going to happen. **Even if you believe that the mortgages on your property add up to more than it's worth, call me anyway.** I have experience putting together deals in these kinds of situations.

Sincerely,

Ralph Roberts

P.S. If you want to save what equity you have left in your home—not to mention your credit rating—doing nothing is *NOT* an option. **Please call me TODAY before it's too late.** Don't let embarrassment about your situation cause you to lose your home with nothing to show for it.

Foreclosure Paper Deal Letter

Send this letter to prospects who own properties that would be good candidates for paper deals.

John and Mary Smith
123 South Avenue
Anywhere, USA

Dear Mr. and Mrs. Smith:

I am sorry to learn that the lender who holds your primary mortgage has begun foreclosing on your home. The worst part is that if you don't do something soon to protect your interests, you will lose your home.

My research also shows that, in addition to the mortgage held by the bank that is already foreclosing, there are additional mortgages and/or liens on your property, and it is quite likely that all of the debts taken together add up to more than the value of your home. If that's the case, **no one could blame you for throwing up your hands in despair and either declaring bankruptcy or simply giving up hope and allowing your home to be sold to the highest bidder at a foreclosure auction.** And unfortunately, even if you do go the bankruptcy route, it's probably just a temporary solution. Because the mortgages are secured by your home, most likely you will eventually have to pay them or lose the house.

I'm writing you this letter to tell you that you don't have to give up hope yet—there may be one more option available to you. All of the mortgage and lien holders in second, third, and lower positions whose interests are junior to the primary mortgage holder face the prospect of losing their investment in your house once the foreclosure is complete. That's because when a bank forecloses on a property, the completion of the foreclosure wipes out all interest in the property held by anyone in a position junior to the defaulted loan. So in some ways, you and the other banks are in the same boat—you are both at risk of losing your investment to the foreclosure.

Many of these second and third mortgage holders, in an attempt to recoup some portion of their investment before it is wiped away by the foreclosure, may be willing to release or assign their liens for less than what is owed. **In essence, the very loans that have handcuffed you up to this point could provide you with the solution to your problems.**

I purchase properties for cash and specialize in negotiating with lien holders to put together these kinds of transactions. But unfortunately, orchestrating this kind of deal is quite time consuming and can easily become complicated. That is why you must realize that, even if the day you'll lose your home is still weeks away, time is already very short. **If we work together, there is a very good chance that you can escape this foreclosure with your credit rating intact, and maybe even some money in your pocket.**

I would be happy to come out to your home and answer any questions you might have. Again, I can't emphasize enough the importance of getting started right away. **Please call me at (810) 555-1234 so we can discuss my program in more detail.**

Sincerely,

Ralph Roberts

P.S. The worst thing you can do now is nothing! I can't be forceful enough on this point. If you ignore this problem, you will lose your home. Please call me today.

Bank REO Letter

This letter is designed to help you get your foot in the door with a bank's REO Department. Send it the first time you contact a particular bank and make sure you have a prospective property in mind on which to make an offer in case they call you back.

Jane Brooks
REO Department
First National Bank
456 East Avenue
Anywhere, USA

Dear Ms. Brooks:

I'm sure you know better than anyone else that the primary business of most banks these days is lending money—not owning property. That is why I've sent you this letter, to propose a partnership that I believe will create a win-win situation for both of us.

If First National is like most other banks I've dealt with, your REO list is full of properties that take up your department's valuable time and resources. I'm also sure that you and your staff have more important things to do than worry about property taxes, maintenance expenses, mandatory waiting periods, and the myriad other headaches that come with bank-owned real estate.

On the other hand, buying, selling, and owning property is *my* business. I have the ability to pay cash for your bank's property and the know-how to make it profitable for both of us. Each piece of real estate First National owns represents valuable resources that could be better spent elsewhere in your institution's operations. I would like to help free up that money so it can be put back to work for you.

I have a particular property in mind that I would like to discuss with you—kind of a way to open the lines of communication between us. I would very much appreciate the opportunity to make a cash offer on this property and others in the future. I will call you soon to talk. In the meantime, if you have any questions, please call me at (810) 555-1234. Thank you for your time and interest.

Sincerely,

Ralph Roberts

Pre-Eviction Letter

Send this letter immediately following your acquisition of the property if there is no redemption period. If there is one, send it upon the completion of the redemption period and change the first sentence of the letter accordingly.

John and Mary Smith
123 South Avenue
Anywhere, USA

Dear Mr. and Mrs. Smith:

As you probably know, your home was sold yesterday at the foreclosure auction at the County Courthouse. My company was the successful bidder that purchased your property from the bank that foreclosed on you.

I'm sorry that you lost your house to foreclosure, but the fact remains that my company now owns the property at **123 South Avenue** and we intend to take possession of it as soon as possible. We don't like evicting people from their homes, but, unfortunately, we are sometimes required to take that sort of action.

I'm writing you this letter to offer you the opportunity to avoid the unpleasantness of an eviction proceeding, which would forcibly remove your family and your possessions from the home. **Please call me by noon on Monday at (810) 555-1234** so we can discuss your situation and I can learn your intentions. If you get my voice mail, please leave me a message with a phone number and a time when I can reach you. If I don't hear from you by noon on Monday, I will be forced to immediately begin the eviction process.

This is an unfortunate situation, but if you will work through it with me, I will do my best to give you ample time to move out of the house. Thank you for your cooperation and immediate attention to this important matter.

Sincerely,

Ralph Roberts

SECTION 3

LANDLORDING

CHAPTER 14

Do You Have the Temperament to Be a Landlord?

It's 2:27 A.M. You're sound asleep in a cozy bed happily dreaming about the next great property you're going to buy, when the shrill ring of the phone next to your bed jerks you awake. Your pulse races as your mind rapidly catalogs all of the horrible things that would have to happen for someone to wake you up at this ungodly hour of the night. With clammy hands, a racing pulse, sweat beads on your brow, and a slight tinge of fear in your heart, you reach for the phone.

"Hello?" you say uneasily.

"Hello," an angry voice shrieks in your ear. "This is Bob, your tenant. The hot water tank's been making noises all night. We thought we should call and let you know." Stifling the urge to hang up the phone and go back to sleep, you grit your teeth and reply in as even a voice as you can muster, "What kind of noises, Bob?"

"I dunno," he says. "It's creaking and moaning like it's gonna explode or something."

You take a deep breath and remind yourself to keep your cool. "Do you really think it's going to blow up, Bob? Or are you exaggerating a little bit?"

"Well . . . ," Bob stammers.

"Do you think it will hold together until the morning when I can get a plumber out to look at it?"

"Don't you want to come out and look at it now?"

You sigh. "Even if I came over there, Bob, I don't have the tools or the know-how to do anything with it. That's why I have a plumber, so he can handle those things. Can I send him over there first thing in the morning?"

Bob's initial anger has drained away. "Yeah," he says quietly. "I guess that would be fine."

"Okay, then," you say with finality. "I'll call him first thing in the morning. Good night."

"Good night," you vaguely hear Bob say as you drop the receiver into the cradle. You roll over and try to get comfortable, determined to get back to that dream. But, as you try to count sheep, all you can seem to count are dollar signs as you turn over in your mind how much this problem is going to cost you. Will the hot water tank need to be replaced? Is there some other problem with the plumbing? Maybe it's nothing major, but there's no way to escape the plumber's bill. It's a pretty sure bet that this is going to kill that unit's cash flow for this month.

Suddenly wide-awake, you resign yourself to the likelihood that you're going to be up for a while and reach for the TV remote. As the picture comes on, you realize that one of the late-night-TV real estate evangelists is hawking his no-money-down, get-rich-quick, real estate acquisition program. A grinning former factory line worker is talking about how he made $23,000 on his first deal without taking any money out of his pocket. The now-rich student and real estate guru amble around a yacht somewhere in the tropics. Everyone on the program laughs, hugs, and weeps with joy over their good fortune. You hit the mute button, cover your head with the pillow, and curse the day you decided to build your wealth through rental properties.

The challenges of owning rental properties

I was probably being a little melodramatic with the preceding story, but make no mistake about it, there are most definitely times when a portfolio of rent-producing properties can feel like a huge weight hanging around your neck. The fact is that, in addition to being a great way to build a huge amount of wealth over time, owning rental properties is often a major pain in the posterior. Even if you escape the midnight phone calls by hiring a property manager to handle your rental portfolio, you will still have your fair share of headaches. Some of the problems that you are likely to face include

- Battles with city rental licensing boards and inspectors
- Tenants who trash your property and still demand their security deposit back
- Vacant rentals creating negative cash flow
- Renters who are habitually late with their rent or who refuse to pay their rent, forcing you to seek eviction in the courts
- Tenants and prospective tenants who bring lawsuits against you
- Costly unexpected major repairs that have to be done NOW
- Public officials and residents who live in your rental neighborhood complaining to you about the behavior of your tenants

Let me emphasize that this list is far from complete!

The benefits of owning rental properties

So, if owning rentals is nothing but bad times and headaches, why do it? You do it because there are few other ways that allow you to slowly and methodically build a great fortune. Being a landlord isn't hip or sexy. In reality, it's rather boring. But it has made more regular people rich than any other investment I know of. That's because few other investments offer the combination of monthly cash flow AND long-term appreciation in value.

There are three main ways in which owning rental properties can be financially rewarding: (1) property value appreciation over time; (2) immediate cash flow; and (3) as a tax shelter that lowers your taxable income.

As I mentioned earlier, the real advantage to owning rental properties comes from building wealth through property value appreciation over time. Cash flow and tax shelters are great tools that can help you pay the bills as your wealth grows. During the first few years you own a property—unless you found an exceptional deal—all or most of the cash flow it generates will go toward paying expenses. However, if you choose properties in strong neighborhoods and you hold onto them for 10–20 years, the cash flow can become phenomenal as rents appreciate and your financial obligations are reduced.

Do you have what it takes?

The reason you don't see books and tapes and late-night infomercials on landlording is because it's not exciting enough for the get-rich-quick crowd. Rentals are all about getting rich *slowly.* But if you don't have what it takes to remain patient and on track, it's not worth getting into. Here are some of the qualities I believe you need to be an effective landlord:

- Patience, patience, patience! You need the patience to wait while your wealth builds over years through property value appreciation. You need the patience to deal with problem tenants without losing your cool. You need the patience to follow local government regulations and federal tax laws that sometimes seem to have been put in place for the sole purpose of discouraging anyone from becoming a landlord.

- A long fuse. In most areas, the city officials, contractors, and other vendors that landlords deal with are a small group in which everyone knows everyone else. If you develop a reputation as a hothead who is difficult to work with, good luck getting any of these people to cooperate with you.
- Cash reserves. It's tough to operate a rental operation on a shoestring. When a furnace blows out or the plumbing springs a leak, your tenant wants (and often needs) it fixed now—and rightfully so. He won't be willing to wait around a week or two while you scrape together the money to get it done. That's one of the reasons why people rent, so they don't have to worry about the problems that come with owning. Those are your problems and you better be prepared to handle them quickly when they arise. Also, the more rental units you own, the more likely it is that you will have vacant properties where you're paying a mortgage note with no income coming in, making a cash reserve absolutely essential.
- Organizational and accounting skills. You need to record and manage incoming rent, security deposits, checking tenants in and out of units, maintenance, repairs, depreciation of the properties, delinquent tenants, and a hundred other things. When you own just one or two units, it isn't a big deal. However, if you build a sizable portfolio, it becomes an increasingly important issue.
- The ability to be "mean" with tenants when necessary. This is a business, after all, and if you want to make money, you will be forced to make business decisions. If your tenant stops paying rent and refuses to leave the property, will you be able to take him or her to court and have him or her forcibly removed from the unit?

Do you have all of these qualities? If not, don't give up yet. If you have the first three characteristics, you can hire people to handle the last two for you. Fortunately for you, there are more resources available to landlords than ever, including property owner associations, published newsletters, comprehensive websites, property-management companies, and Internet forums and discussion groups. Seeking out and utilizing these types of groups and services can significantly shorten your learning curve. I'll discuss all of them and more in upcoming chapters.

Summary

As you consider investing in rental properties, take an honest look at yourself and see if you have what it takes to build wealth through landlording. And before you invest your retirement account or the kids' college funds on a rental property, be fully aware of what you're getting yourself into. Being a landlord is a great method for building wealth, but it's not for everyone.

CHAPTER 15

Managing Your Properties

Once you own several rental properties, someone has to manage them. When you first start out and you only own one or two properties, it's not too difficult to manage them on your own. But as the number of units in your portfolio grows, keeping a handle on everything can become more and more difficult, especially when several units experience maintenance and tenant problems at once while leases are coming up for renewal in a few others and the ads you placed on several vacant units just don't seem to be drawing applicants, and . . . Well, I guess you see my point.

Property management resources

The two best ways to ease your management burden are to purchase and implement property-management software for your home computer or to hire a property manager to step in and manage the units for you. The software is a one-time expense (until upgrades are released) that will help you get more organized and efficient. The property manager is an ongoing cost that will cut into your cash flow, but it will also free you from the daily tasks of taking care of your rental properties to perhaps seek out and acquire additional houses.

Property-Management Software

When you purchase property-management software, your license will normally allow you to apply the program to a limited number of units. As your rental portfolio grows, you will be required to upgrade your license to allow more units on the program. Most software does offer a license for an unlimited number of units, but those can be quite expensive. I've seen decent property management software range from $20—for a basic program that includes just three units—up to several thousand dollars for a comprehensive program with unlimited properties. You can probably find the basic programs at a computer or office superstore or on the Internet. For more advanced software, you may have to join a local landlord club or property-management trade organization. I can't tell you which program will be right for you; that's something you'll have to decide for yourself. However, here are some of the features you should look for in a property-management program:

- ❑ Tenant database that includes
  - Name and phone number
  - Address of unit rented
  - Employer name and phone number
  - Monthly rent and due date
  - Amount of security deposit
  - Emergency contact name and phone number
  - Past landlords and residences
  - Lease start and end dates
  - Rental history—late payments, neighbor complaints, etc.

- ❑ Property database that includes
  - Photos of units
  - Tenant and rent of occupied units
  - Market rental value of vacant units
  - Depreciation of property
  - Scheduled maintenance
  - Maintenance history
  - Property-specific "For Rent" advertisements
  - Holders of any liens or mortgage notes on the property
    - ✓ Payment amounts and due dates
  - Tax and insurance costs and due dates
- ❑ Vendor database that includes
  - Name, address, and phone number
  - Service category
  - Job history—work completed, quoted price and time, actual cost, and time frame, etc.
  - Outstanding work orders
- ❑ Accounting features, including
  - Accounts payable reports
  - Accounts receivable reports
  - Complete balance sheets
  - Cash flow reports and forecasts
  - Income and expense reports covering:
    - ✓ The entire portfolio
    - ✓ Each individual unit
  - Maintenance expense reports, covering:
    - ✓ The entire portfolio
    - ✓ Each individual unit
    - ✓ Each individual vendor

- Delinquency reports
- Tenant statements

❑ Reminders or flags that alert you to

- Overdue rent payments
- Maintenance jobs past the scheduled date of completion
- Upcoming lease expiration dates
- Regularly scheduled maintenance
- Due dates of property mortgage, tax, and insurance payments

❑ Self-generating documents, including

- Property inspection reports
- Work orders
- 1099 statements for vendors
- Letters addressing:
  - ✓ Overdue rent
  - ✓ Complaints against the tenant
  - ✓ Upcoming scheduled maintenance
  - ✓ Lease renewal
- Tenant and vendor mailing labels

Chances are that you will not find a single software package that contains all of these features unless you are examining the most expensive programs. Look for flexibility. If it doesn't come loaded with the self-generating documents, does it have the capacity for you to enter templates and generate your own letters and reports? If the databases aren't complete, do they at least have miscellaneous space that you can customize to meet your needs?

Spend some time researching software programs before spending the money on one. It helps to run your rental business for a while without software or with a demo program so you can get firsthand knowledge of the kinds of features that will be important to you. Other landlords are also a good source for the pros and cons associated with different programs.

Property-Management Firms

After reviewing all of the accounting and regular tasks associated with managing your own property, you may decide that it's well worth the expense to let someone else handle all of that stuff for you. Property-management firms can oversee everything from advertising for a new tenant to evicting nonpaying renters and everything in between. In researching property-management firms, look at what services are offered and decide which responsibilities you want to give up and which you'd prefer keeping control of yourself.

Property-management companies generally charge a percentage of monthly gross rent—normally 5–15 percent—for their services. Some may also have an additional flat fee for finding new tenants. Others charge a flat monthly rate for property owners with just a few rental units in their portfolios. No matter what the monthly fee, the landlord is always responsible for paying expenses such as maintenance, advertising, and legal expenses associated with evictions.

The following is a list of many of the features and services offered by property-management companies. Before you hire a firm to manage your properties, decide which services are important to you.

- Licensed real estate broker. Many states require property managers to have a broker's license.
- Computerized record keeping. This allows your rep to have easy access to your account information.
- Payment of bills and mortgages for property owner
- Writing and placement of rental advertisements

- Thorough screening of prospective tenants, including
  - ✓ Credit report
  - ✓ Check of legal records
  - ✓ Employment verification
  - ✓ Reference checks
- Negotiating and executing leases
- Handling security deposit escrow accounts
- Itemized property inspections at tenant move-in and move-out
- Collection of rent and dealing with delinquent tenants
- Handling evictions of nonpayers
- Reporting tenant delinquencies and evictions to credit bureaus
- Timely payment of rental income to unit owner
- Maintaining market rental value with regular rent increases as leases expire and are renewed
- Taking care of all maintenance issues, including getting competitive bids and owner approval before commencing work on larger jobs
- Seven-day, 24-hour access to property manager by both tenant and property owner
- Listing and selling properties for owner, if requested

If you choose a good firm that does everything listed here, the extent of your contact with them should be a monthly check and report and a call for approval before they undertake any special expenses. As with the property-management software, do your research and seek the advice of your peers before signing on with any company. Just because a firm is established and successful does not necessarily mean that it's right for you. Sometimes, smaller players—like a landlord with fewer than 20 rental units—can get lost in the shuffle because of his account's relative unimportance to the property manager when compared to bigger accounts with hundreds or even thousands of units in its portfolio. No matter which firm you choose, make sure they will provide you with regular written accounting, and be sure to learn the company's chain of command so you know whom to call if you are ever unhappy with your account representative's performance.

OTHER PROPERTY-MANAGEMENT OPTIONS

Many smaller portfolio rental owners find that they get better service from an individual rather than a big company. There are individual property managers who manage units for smaller investors who may own only a handful of properties. By turning your rentals over to one of these individuals, you can become a big player and one of his most important clients rather quickly as you build your inventory.

Another way to raise your clout is by creating an alliance with several small-to-midsize property owners so you can all choose a property manager as a block. This will make your group more valuable to the property manager, and it could lower expenses for all of you. If you have enough properties in your alliance, you could even hire an individual to manage just your group's inventory.

Summary

As your rental property portfolio grows, it will become more challenging to manage your properties. To ease your management burden, you can purchase and implement property-management software. Carefully review the available programs to see if they offer the tools you need. At first, you may want to find a basic program and upgrade to a more sophisticated (and more costly) one as your portfolio grows. Another approach to easing your management burden is to hire a property manager. Although this will cut into your cash flow, this can be more than offset by the additional time you'll have to pursue new acquisitions. Whichever approach you choose, don't wait too long to address this important issue. Things can get out of hand quite easily if you don't have a solid property-management system in place.

CHAPTER 16

Selecting the Right Tenants Is Key to Your Success

Few things can turn your rental business into a nightmare more quickly than bad tenants can. Renting to the wrong people can cost you an enormous amount of time, money, and stress. Although you can never totally insulate yourself from this potential problem, you can take steps to weed out many potentially disastrous prospects. Finding tenants who remain in the property for years on end, pay their rent on time, and keep your unit in good condition can go a long way to helping you build a strong-performing rental portfolio, and it can make owning rental properties a fun and easy way to build wealth.

Finding tenants through personal contacts

The best place to find quality tenants is through referrals from people you trust such as friends, family, and social and business acquaintances. Let those in your sphere of influence know what type of property you have available and tell them you'd appreciate it if they let you know about any prospective renters. When they bring you someone, draw a character reference out of them by asking, "If you owned this property, would you feel comfortable renting to this person?" Listen to their answer and pay close attention to their reaction to the question. Of course, you won't be able to fill every vacancy this way, so you'll still have to rely on other approaches, such as advertising.

Finding tenants through classified advertising

The most common method of attracting prospective tenants remains the classified section of your local newspaper. In addition to this old standby, there are now also plenty of websites where you can place your ad with little or no cost. Take advantage of all these outlets.

In writing your ad for tenants, include the best features of your property. Some good examples include:

- 3-bedroom, 2-bath house, with full finished basement, just minutes away from restaurants, shopping, and I-696.
- 2-bedroom, 1-bath condo, newly remodeled, new paint and carpet throughout. Like new.
- 2 bed, 1-1/2 bath house, large back deck and yard. At $715 a month, rent is 15% less than comparable rentals in the area.

Be creative in your ad writing. If price of rent is not one of your top selling points, don't include it in the ad. That will give prospective renters a chance to fall in love with your property before you spring the rent on them.

Determining your asking price

Before starting your search for tenants, whether through word of mouth or through advertising, check out the rental inventory in your marketplace. Examine how other property owners construct their advertisements. If possible, get a look at the actual properties and talk to other landlords about their rent structure. Try to remain emotionally detached from the process of setting your rent. You may be tempted to work backwards—that is, by first figuring out how much you need to cover your expenses, but your own monthly payments on the unit should have absolutely no bearing on the actual rent. Only the marketplace can determine what a unit will rent for.

In determining your pricing, the ideal approach would be as follows: "Three similar units in the same neighborhood just rented for an average of $610 per month, and there are other similar vacancies nearby asking $625 or less, so I will ask for $600–$615. That way, I'll get my vacancy filled more quickly." If you're tempted to take the reverse approach and think, "Let's see, I have to pay $425 a month on principal, interest, taxes, and insurance, and I want to make $200 in cash flow each month, so I'll set the rent at $625 per month," then take a minute and figure out what it will cost you for each month your rental sits vacant. For example, at a rental value of $600, if your unit is unoccupied for just one month because of your inflated rent demands, you will lose an average of $50 per month over the length of a one-year lease. When you look at it that way, doesn't it seem a little silly to hold out for $625 when you've got a prospect who's willing to move in for $600? And if your rent demands are inflated, you run the risk of a vacancy extending beyond a single month, further destroying your cash flow.

The Federal Fair Housing Act

Before you advertise your rental property, you should have a bit of knowledge about the Federal Fair Housing Act of 1968. The act prohibits housing discrimination on the basis of race, color, national origin, religion, sex, familial status, or disability. The act was amended in 1988 to offer additional protection to people with disabilities, stating that a landlord may NOT refuse to allow a tenant with a disability to make reasonable modifications to the rental dwelling or common use areas. The landlord is not required to pay for these changes, and he may, when reasonable, permit the modifications only if the tenant agrees to restore the rental unit to its original state before moving out. Additionally, the landlord may NOT refuse to make reasonable accommodations in rules, policies, practices, or services if required by the disabled tenant. For example, although it is perfectly legitimate for you to have a "No Pets" policy in your rental properties, you would still have to allow a blind person to keep a Seeing-Eye dog in the unit.

The act also says you may NOT use obviously discriminatory words in any advertising or marketing. Many landlords run into trouble by unwittingly using the wrong words or phrases in their ads for tenants. When you put an ad together, scrutinize it for words or phrases that refer to race, color, national origin, religion, sex, familial status, or disability. For instance, you can't say the rental is located in a nice "family neighborhood," or your one-bedroom condo would make a great "bachelor pad," or the area is "populated by many Christians." Any language that seems to deter one of the protected classes from answering your ad can be viewed as discriminatory by the Fair Housing Act. Saying "family neighborhood" could be seen as implying that singles or people without children are unwelcome. Some things you might innocently perceive as selling points could actually be seen as violations of the Federal Fair Housing Act. And believe me, getting caught violating that law is serious business that you don't want to experience. If you have doubts about whether a word or phrase should be used, do yourself a favor and either consult with your lawyer or simply omit the questionable word or phrase.

You can find out more about the Federal Fair Housing Act on the HUD website at www.hud.gov/fairhsg1.html.

As you start interviewing tenants and showing them your property, you can protect yourself again from accusations of violating this law by systematizing your tenant-screening process. Follow this process the exact same way every time and it will be tough for any prospective tenant to prove any discrimination on your part. Have every potential renter fill out an application upon arriving to see the property. If a prospective tenant refuses to fill it out, you probably wouldn't want that person renting from you anyway, because it's likely that he or she either has something to hide or is simply window-shopping with no real interest in renting the unit.

In showing a rental unit to potential renters, share with them the price and terms you're asking for. Make sure you offer the same price and terms to every single prospect that comes through the door. Adjusting your price based on your impressions of the candidate will get you into hot water faster than you can say "Federal Fair Housing Act." It wouldn't hurt to present interested renters with the price and terms in writing so there is no mistaking what rate you were asking if a complaint ever materializes against you.

Screening potential tenants

Once a prospect has been informed of the rental terms and expresses interest in the rental unit, don't finalize any arrangements until you've thoroughly screened your applicant. First, ask to see a photo ID to make sure the person is who she says she is. Then explain that you will need to check references before signing the lease. I recommend that you pass onto the potential tenants as an application fee any costs associated with your credit check, such as a credit report and/or legal records check. If you don't pass this expense on to applicants, you're looking at $15 to $50 coming out of your pocket for each prospect that gets serious. In addition to covering your expenses, the application fee suddenly causes the prospect to have a financial stake in the situation, further separating the window-shoppers from those serious about moving into a property.

Invest the half hour or so it takes to check your prospect's references, verify employment, and call current and former landlords. However, when calling the current landlord, take whatever he or she says with a grain of salt. If your possible renter is in fact a nightmare tenant, a current landlord might be willing to lie to his own mother to get the renter out of his property. Finally, be sure to check your prospect's credit standing. To get access to a prospect's credit report, check on the web at landlord resource sites or call your area's property owners' association for advice.

Utility costs

If your prospect's references and credit reports come back favorable, it's time to sit down, sign the lease, collect a security deposit and first month's rent, and set a schedule for move-in and switching of utilities into your new renter's name.

Whenever possible, have your tenants cover their own utilities. This protects you from the expense of excessive use, keeps you out of the middle of any disputes between the utility companies and your tenant, and saves you the headache of requesting a rent increase to cover unexpected utility costs. The only times I would consider going against this rule of thumb is when it's just not possible, as in the case of a duplex where both units share the same furnace and/or hot water tank, or when the utility becomes a lien against the property when not paid. In Michigan, for instance, water bills are considered the responsibility of the homeowner, so even if a tenant is supposed to pay them, they become the owner's problem if the tenant doesn't pay them, because the amount owed is recorded with the Register of Deeds as a lien against the property. The homeowner cannot sell or refinance that property until the water bill is addressed. I still have my renters cover the water bills, but I require proof that it's been paid—either by paying it myself and having tenants reimburse me, or by having them show me a receipt or a copy of their cancelled check as proof that they paid it.

Government-subsidized tenants

A completely different approach to filling your vacancies is to seek out government-subsidized renters. There are various programs around the country, but the most common and well-funded one is called the Section 8 Program.

Funded by HUD and run by state agencies—usually the State Housing Development Authority—Section 8 provides vouchers to individuals and families whose annual income falls in the "extremely low" or "very low" categories according to HUD guidelines. The program was set up so low-income families and individuals could secure housing that was decent, safe, and sanitary. The tenant is expected to contribute 30 percent of the household's monthly-adjusted income and the Section 8 Program pays the rest. What makes being a Section 8 landlord attractive to many rental property owners is that it's a good way to keep units rented with a guarantee that they will receive the majority of the rent on time every month, paid directly to the landlord by the government agency administering the program. The drawback is that there are no guarantees about the actual tenant's share of the rent.

There are certain guidelines that a property and landlord must meet in order to be considered for the program. The best way to learn more about Section 8 and other government subsidy programs and to see whether or not you qualify to participate is to contact the local office of your state's Housing Development Authority.

Summary

In order for your rental business to flourish, you must take steps to avoid choosing bad tenants who are consistently delinquent in paying their rent or who damage your property. Be sure to carefully screen all applicants. Before starting your search for tenants, whether through word of mouth or through advertising, check out the rental inventory in your marketplace and be sure you are not pricing yourself out of the market. Also, pay careful attention to the rules set by the Fair Housing Act to avoid being in violation of it and the perception that you're discriminating against certain individuals or groups. If you're willing to accept government-subsidized tenants (Section 8s), you can be guaranteed a timely payment of a large portion of the rent each month. The drawback is that tenants may not be so conscientious about their portion of the rent.

CHAPTER 17

Essential Landlord Resources

Landlords today have more resources at their disposal than ever before. With property owners associations, the Internet, and published educational materials and newsletters, practically everything you need to build and manage a successful rental portfolio is just a phone call or mouse click away.

Online resources

The amount of information about landlording available on the web is staggering. To access some of this information, go to your favorite search engine, type in "Landlord Resources," and let the fun begin. In addition to websites created by real estate experts, landlord-service providers, and other property owners, you can find landlording news and discussion groups, bulletin boards, chat rooms, and ListServs, through which you can share information with others who have experience in a particular subject—in this case, landlording.

The following list offers some online resources that you may find helpful, along with a brief description of each. However, bear in mind that, because the Internet is constantly changing, these may not be the most current or best resources available; they are simply ones that looked promising at the time of the writing of this book. Some of them may be gone or moved to a new address by the time this book is published. That's the danger of putting web addresses in a book. Further, I can't make any assurances that the information on these sites is 100 percent complete and accurate. As always, when in doubt, consult your attorney.

General real estate information

- www.relibrary.com—Provides real estate industry news and resources

Resources specifically for landlords

- www.mrlandlord.com—Offers "free and low cost online resources for the do-it-yourself rental property owner" and offers the MrLandlord Newsletter
- www.landlord.com—Comprehensive site that features forms, letters, articles, news, and more
- www.cses.com/rental—Has a little of everything: forms, advice, tax law, property acquisition, and more

Landlord–tenant law information

- www.mv.com/ipusers/nhpoa/other.htm—Provides landlord–tenant statutes from all 50 states
- www.nolo.com/encyclopedia/lt_ency.html—Offers free information about many landlord–tenant issues

Real Estate Investment Newsgroups and Chat Rooms

- www.real-estate-online.com—Focuses on real estate investment, no-money-down and paper deals, and creative financing
- alt.invest.real-estate—Once you sift through all of the spam, this is a decent Newsgroup.

Off-line resources

While the Internet can be a terrific resource, in my opinion, nothing beats networking in person with other people who do the same thing as you. Local and regional property owners associations offer you the chance to learn about local rental issues. In addition, as a group, you can band together to get lower cost products and services and can use the strength of your numbers to be heard on the local political scene. But the best thing about being a part of these groups is the social interaction, the opportunity to spend time with people with the same interests as you, discuss issues affecting landlords, and swap war stories. It's during this one-on-one time that you can discuss the pros and cons of property-management firms and software with other landlords. And it is through these relationships that you can discover entire portfolios of great rental properties—through a friend and fellow landlord who has decided to call it quits, for example.

The Benefits of Membership

When you join a property owners association, you will have the opportunity to learn about the many aspects of property ownership and landlording much more quickly than you could learn on your own. Of course, some organizations are more active than others and offer more services to their members. More active groups are likely to organize more meetings and provide better educational resources, such as presenting guest speakers with expertise in specific areas of property ownership. Some issues that you can expect to be addressed at association meetings include

- City codes and enforcement
- Property acquisition
- Contractor licensing issues
- Local landlord–tenant statutes
- Lead-based paint rules and regulations
- The Federal Fair Housing Act of 1968
- Landlord income-tax issues
- Tenant relations
- How to collect from delinquent tenants more effectively
- Eviction procedures

In addition to education and discussion, your property owners association can also give you access to forms such as leases, addendums, and tenant applications and can provide services such as credit reports, reference checks, and evictions. Most of these groups also keep a resource library stocked with books, tapes, and other educational materials for use by members.

At least two of the websites mentioned here—www.landlord.com and www.mv.com/ipusers/nhpoa/other.htm—contain listings of property owners associations across the country.

Summary

As a landlord, you have many responsibilities; and as a landlord working to build a successful real estate portfolio, you will need to tap all the resources available to you to make your work easier. The good news is that there are many resources, including property owners associations, the Internet, and published educational materials and newsletters. Often you'll find that everything you need to build and manage a successful rental portfolio is just a phone call or mouse click away.

CHAPTER 18

The Tools of the Successful Landlord

When you own rental properties, your tenants will only be as strong as your screening process. Having each prospect fill out a complete rental application and actually checking their credit report and references (as explained in Chapter 16) will allow you to filter out 85 percent of the undesirable applicants.

In this chapter you will find all of the general forms I use on my own rentals. It's a smart idea to have your attorney look over these documents—especially the lease—before you use any of them as landlord–tenant law can vary dramatically from state to state. Your lawyer is best equipped to determine what additional steps, if any, you should take to ensure thorough legal protection for yourself. As you will see, some of the forms in this chapter include clauses specific to Michigan. You should take the time to find out what clauses are needed in your state.

As you review the forms that follow, when you get to the lease you'll notice that it contains a discount for tenants who pay their rent on time or early as well as a penalty for those who are late. I've found this approach to be extremely useful in getting tenants to pay their rent on time. Although most people have good intentions about paying their rent on time, when the late fee doesn't kick in until the 5th of the month, even the most conscientious of tenants will sometimes take advantage of the cushion between when the rent is actually due and when the late fee is added. By offering a monetary incentive to pay on or before the 1st, my organization has significantly cut down the number of renters who pay between the 1st and the 5th. As you tailor the details of the lease to your particular situation, you may consider a similar approach to reducing the number of late rent payments.

Rental Application Checklist

Property Address: ______________________________________

____

Prospective Tenant Name(s): ______________________________

The following steps must be completed before a lease is offered:

- ❑ Complete Rental Application
- ❑ Obtain Credit Report
- ❑ Collect Following items:
  - ✓ Two years tax returns
  - ✓ Two months bank statements
  - ✓ Last three pay stubs
  - ✓ Copy of driver's license
- ❑ Provide tenant with Lead-Based Paint booklet—if house was built before 1978
- ❑ Fill out and have tenant initial Lead-Based Paint disclosure (For more information on this issue and how it affects you as a landlord, visit the National Lead Information Center at www.epa.gov/lead/nlic.htm)
- ❑ Submit file for credit approval

Once the tenant is approved, complete the following steps:

- ❑ Explain and complete Lease
- ❑ Collect Security Deposit and first and last months' rent
- ❑ Have tenant sign one copy of Commencement Inventory Checklist and keep it in file. (Tenant takes two copies, fills them out and signs them, and returns one copy to you.)
- ❑ Remind tenant about discount for paying rent on time or early and the date when next rent payment is due

Rental Application

One application should be filled out for <u>each</u> person whose name will be on the lease.

Property Address: (to be filled out by landlord) ______________________

____

Personal Information:

Name of Applicant: ______________ Social Security #: ______________

Home Phone: ________ Work Phone: ________ Other Phone: ________

Current Address: ______________________________________

____

Years lived there:__________ Reason for moving: ________________

Previous Address: ______________________________________

____

Years lived there:__________ Reason for moving: ________________

Employment Information:

Employer: __________________________ Years with company:________

Address: ____

Supervisor: ________________________ Phone: ______________

Position:___________________________ Base Salary: ______________

Previous Employer:___________________ Years with company:________

Address: ____

Supervisor: ________________________ Phone: ______________

Position:___________________________ Base Salary: ______________

Reason for leaving: ______________________________________

Questions:

If you answer "Yes" to any of the following questions, please provide details, including dates.

Have you ever filed for bankruptcy? ______________________________

____

Have you ever been evicted or asked to leave a rental property? __________

____

Financial Information:

Bank Name: ______________________ Branch: ______________

Type of Account: ____________________ Acct. # ________________

All Other Financial Obligations (use back of application if necessary)

Creditor Name	Address	Phone	Monthly Payment

References:

Current Landlord: ____________________ Phone: ________________

Previous Landlord: ____________________ Phone: ________________

Personal Reference #1: ________________ Years Known: ___________

Relationship: ________________________ Phone: ________________

Personal Reference #2: ________________ Years Known: ___________

Relationship: ________________________ Phone: ________________

Personal Reference #3: ________________ Years Known: ___________

Relationship: ________________________ Phone: ________________

In Case of Emergency, Notify:

Name	Address	Phone	Relationship
1.)			
2.)			

Authorization:

By signing below, I hereby authorize the landlord or his agent to request and review a copy of my credit report and credit history. I also agree, upon request, to furnish the landlord or his agent with additional credit references. I further represent that all of the information provided in this application is true and accurate to the best of my knowledge. I realize that future discovery that I knowingly misrepresented myself on this application could be grounds for immediate rejection of my application or immediate eviction if the false information led to me becoming a tenant.

______________________________________ ________________

Applicant Signature *Date*

LEASE

This Lease is made this __________ day of __________, 20_____ by and between _____________ (Landlord) and _____________ (Tenant).

In consideration of the mutual covenants herein contained Landlord and Tenant agree as follows:

1. LEASED PREMISES

Landlord leases to Tenant(s), and Tenant(s) hires from Landlord, on the terms and subject to the conditions herein contained, these premises situated in the City of _____________, County of ____________, State of ____________, commonly known as ____________________________ (Street Address).

2. TERM

The term of this Lease shall commence on ____________________, and shall continue until midnight on ____________________. Tenant(s) may elect to terminate the Lease upon thirty (30) days' notice to Landlord and payment of $_____________ by Tenant(s) to terminate the Lease.

3. RENT

The Tenant(s) hereby agree(s) to hire the above-described premises and to pay at a total of _____________ dollars for the full Lease period, said sum to be paid in monthly installments of $_____________ each, due on or before the FIRST day of each month. A total of $_____________, to cover the first and final monthly installments prescribed by this Lease is due and payable by the Tenant(s) upon the signing of this Lease.

If said rent payments are received by Landlord on or before the FIRST of each month, Tenant(s) shall receive a $25.00 discount for that month's rent and said total amount owed for the full Lease period shall be reduced accordingly. Payment must be received and in possession of the Landlord on or before the first of each month. Payments that are mailed on the FIRST or are delayed by the Post Office or for any reason will not qualify for said discount. Payments that are returned to Landlord due to insufficient funds or that cannot be processed by the bank, shall not qualify for said discount. Payment shall be made to Landlord or his authorized agent at:

____

____

____

____

Or at such other place as Landlord may designate from time to time.

4. LATE PAYMENT CHARGES

In the event that rent payments are not received by Landlord by the close of business on the 5th day of the month in which they are due, a charge of $25.00 will be assessed as additional rent, with an additional rental charge of $2.00 per day for each day rent payments are not made thereafter. If not paid with rent, such charges may be deducted from the unused portion of the security deposit.

5. RETURNED PAYMENTS

Any check tendered by Tenant to Landlord for payment of rent or other charges assessed in connection with the terms of the Lease Agreement that is returned by Tenant's bank to Landlord for insufficient funds, or if Landlord must return the check to Tenant because it cannot be processed, an additional rental charge of $20.00 will be assessed the Tenant for that month's rent. If not paid with rent, such charges may be deducted from the unused portion of the security deposit.

6. NON-REFUNDABLE CLEANING FEE

Tenant(s) hereby pay(s) to Landlord a non-refundable cleaning fee in the amount of ______________________ for the purpose of CLEANING THE WALLS, APPLIANCES, FLOORS, WINDOWS, AND DRAPES upon vacating of the Premises so that they are in the same condition as of the signing of this Agreement. THIS IS NOT PART OF THE SECURITY DEPOSIT.

7. UTILITIES

Tenant(s) shall be responsible for and pay all utility bills in respect of the Premises during the term, except the ___________________________, which shall be the responsibility of the Landlord.

8. USE OF PREMISES

(A) Tenant(s) shall not use, or allow any person or persons to use said Premises for any purpose in violation of the laws of the State of __________________, the United States, and/or the City of ________________, or any lawful authority.

(B) The Premises shall be used only as a single-family residence and for no other purpose. No more than ________________________ adults and __________________ children shall reside in the Premises.

(C) Tenant(s) shall not cause or permit any noise or nuisance whatsoever on the Premises.

9. PETS

No pets of any kind shall be kept or brought on the Premises. If this provision is violated by Tenant(s), Tenant(s) agree(s) to pay the sum of ______________________ per month for each month said provision is violated.

10. HOUSE RULES

Tenant(s) agree(s) to abide by all house rules concerning the Premises whether promulgated before or after the execution of this Lease. By way of example, but not limitation, house rules may be passed relating to noise, odors, disposal of refuse, parking, and use of common areas. Landlord shall convey any house rules to Tenant(s) in writing.

11. TELEPHONE INSTALLATION

Tenant(s) agree(s) that within ______________________________ days after the date this Lease is to commence, Tenant(s) shall install and have operating, at Tenant's expense, a telephone on the Premises. Tenant(s) shall maintain the telephone for the entire duration of this Lease and shall be responsible for all bills incurred, including any for disconnection of said phone upon Tenant(s) vacating said Premises. Tenant(s) shall provide Landlord as soon as possible a telephone number for the Premises.

12. ASSIGNMENT AND SUBLETTING

Tenant shall not assign this Lease in whole or in part, or sublet all or any portion of the Premises.

13. CONDITION OF PREMISES; ALTERATION; MAINTENANCE; REPAIRS

(A) By executing this Lease, Tenant(s) accept(s) the Premises in their existing condition and acknowledge that the Premises are in good order and repair, except as Tenant may indicate on the Commencement Inventory Checklist, duplicate copies of which are supplied by Landlord as required by law and attached hereto.

(B) Tenant(s) shall maintain the Premises in a clean and sanitary condition and shall surrender the Premises at the termination of this Lease in as good a condition as when received, ordinary wear and tear excepted. Tenant(s) shall not paint, paper, or otherwise redecorate the Premises, or make any alterations to the Premises whatsoever, without the prior written consent of the Landlord. Tenant(s) shall commit no waste on the Premises.

(C) Tenant(s) agree(s) to be responsible for any damage caused to the Premises by him or his family members, guests or invitees, and further agrees to promptly report to Landlord any damage caused to or discovered in the Premises. Landlord, at his option, may, upon discovery of damage to the Premises, make such repairs as are necessary to restore the Premises to their original condition, and Tenant(s) shall reimburse the Landlord for the total cost of any such repairs for which he is responsible hereunder.

(D) Landlord and Tenant(s) each hereby release the other, including employees, agents, family members, invitees, and guests of the other, from all liability arising from loss, damage or injury caused by fire or other casualty to the extent of any recovery by the injured party under a policy of insurance which permits waiver of liability and waives the insured party under a policy of insurance which permits waiver of liability and waives the insurer's rights of subrogation.

14. INSPECTION

Landlord, or his agent, shall have the right to enter the Premises at any reasonable time and upon any reasonable notice for the purpose of inspecting the Premises, showing the Premises to prospective residents or purchasers, or for the purpose of making necessary repairs. In the event of an emergency, Landlord shall be permitted to enter the Premises without notice for any reasonable purpose connected with the emergency.

15. INDEMNIFICATION

Landlord shall not be liable for any damage or injury occurring on or about the Premises to Tenant(s), his family members, guests or invitees, or to any personal property whatsoever that may be on the Premises, except in the case of the Landlord's failure to perform, or negligent performance of, a duty. Tenant(s) shall hold Landlord harmless from and agrees to indemnify and defend Landlord against any and all loss, costs, expenses, damage or liability (including attorney's fees) arising out of any accident, claim, demand, suit, action, or other occurrence on the Premises or any person or property whomsoever or whatsoever, no matter how caused, except in the case of the Landlord's failure to perform or negligent performance of a duty imposed by law.

16. POSSESSION

Tenant(s) shall have possession of the Premises on the day of the commencement of the term. If, however, Landlord is unable to deliver possession of the Premises on that date, Landlord shall not be liable for any damages caused thereby, nor shall this Agreement be void or voidable, but rent shall abate until possession is delivered. If possession is not delivered within ten (10) days of the commencement of the term of this Lease, either Landlord or Tenant(s) may, by written notice, terminate this agreement.

17. DEFAULT

(A) Tenant's failure to pay rent when due, or to perform any of its obligations hereunder, shall constitute as a default. If a default occurs, Landlord may, at its option, terminate this Lease and regain possession of the Premises in accordance with applicable law. If Tenant(s) shall be absent from the Premises for a period of five consecutive days while in default, Tenant(s) shall, at Landlord's option, be deemed to have abandoned the Premises. Recovery of the Premises by Landlord shall be permitted to accelerate the rent due throughout the term of this Lease and demand immediate payment thereof. Tenant(s) may not be liable for the total accelerated amount of rent due hereunder because of Landlord's obligation to minimize damages through attempted re-renting of the Premises.

(B) In the event of a default, it is understood that either party to this Agreement has the right to have a court determine the actual amount due and owing the other.

(C) Neither party to this Lease shall be liable for legal costs of attorney's fees incurred by the other in connection with a dispute arising hereunder except that such costs of fees are specifically permitted by statute.

18. WAIVER

Landlord's failure to enforce any term of this Lease shall not be deemed a waiver of the enforcement of that or any other term, nor shall any acceptance of a partial payment of rent be deemed a waiver of Landlord's right to full amount thereof.

19. NOTICES

Any notice which either party may, or is required, to give hereunder may be served personally or sent by first-class mail, postage prepaid, as follows:

(A) To Tenant(s) at Premises;

(B) To Landlord at: ______________________________
____
____

Or other places as may be designated in writing by the parties from time to time.

20. HOLDING OVER

Any holding over after the expiration of the term of this Lease, unless pursuant to the express written consent of the Landlord, shall be construed as a month-to-month tenancy, which shall be governed by all applicable terms of this Lease, except that the rent shall be twice the amount hereinbefore stated.

21. SECURITY DEPOSIT

Upon execution of this Agreement, Tenant(s) shall deposit with Landlord, the sum of ____________ dollars, which shall be held by Landlord as a security deposit for the faithful performance by Tenant(s) of his obligation hereunder. This security deposit shall be returned to Tenant(s) upon termination of this Lease and surrender by Tenant(s) of the Premises, subject, but not limited to, the following conditions.

(A) There shall be no damage to the leased Premises beyond ordinary wear and tear;

(B) All rent due and payable under the terms of this Lease shall be paid to Landlord;

(C) All keys shall have been returned to Landlord;

(D) All debris, rubbish and discards shall have been placed in proper rubbish containers;

(E) All late charges and service charges for bad checks, if any, shall have been paid; and

(F) Tenant shall have left a forwarding address with Landlord.

Michigan law provides that:

You must notify your Landlord in writing within four (4) days after you move of a forwarding address where you can be reached and where you will receive mail; otherwise your Landlord shall be relieved of sending you an itemized list of damages and the penalties adherent to that failure.

The security deposit, less any deductions, with an itemized list of damages, shall be returned to Tenant(s) within 30 days of any termination of this Lease. IT IS SPECIFICALLY UNDERSTOOD THAT THE AFORESAID SECURITY DEPOSIT SHALL NOT BE CONSIDERED PREPAID RENTAL AND SHALL NOT BE APPLIED BY TENANT ON THE LAST MONTH'S RENT. Tenant's security deposit will be held by __________________________.

22. FIRST AND LAST MONTHS' RENT

In addition to the above mentioned security deposit, Landlord acknowledges receipt of the sum of ____________________________ as the first and last months' rent.

23. SEVERABILITY

In the event that any part of this Agreement shall be held invalid, the remainder thereof shall remain in full force and effect.

24. FIRE OR DESTRUCTION

If the Premises, or any other substantial part thereof, shall be destroyed by fire or other casualty so as to render them untenantable, either Landlord or Tenant shall have the right to terminate this Lease upon written notice.

25. ENTIRE AGREEMENT

The foregoing constitutes the entire agreement between the parties and may not be modified except in writing, signed by both parties.

26. TRUTH IN RENTING

NOTICE: MICHIGAN LAW ESTABLISHES RIGHTS AND OBLIGATIONS FOR THE PARTIES TO RENTAL AGREEMENTS. THIS AGREEMENT IS REQUIRED TO COMPLY WITH THE TRUTH-IN-RENTING ACT. IF YOU HAVE A QUESTION ABOUT THE INTERPRETATION OR LEGALITY OF A PROVISION OF THIS AGREEMENT, YOU MAY WISH TO SEEK ASSISTANCE FROM A LAWYER OR OTHER QUALIFIED PERSON.

27. SHOWING OF PREMISES

TENANT WILL PERMIT SHOWING OF PREMISES FOR THE PURPOSE OF SALE. LANDLORD SHALL GIVE NOTICE OF SUCH SHOWINGS.

IN WITNESS HEREOF, the undersigned have executed this Lease as of the date first written above.

____________________	____________________
WITNESS	LANDLORD
	____________________
	LANDLORD
____________________	____________________
WITNESS	TENANT
	____________________
	TENANT

Commencement Inventory Checklist

(Page 1 of 2)

Note the condition of the rental property by completing this checklist, which shows what claims were chargeable to the last prior tenants. Please examine the physical condition of your rental unit and report your findings on this form to your landlord within 7 days. You will be responsible for any damages not reported on this form. Items not specifically set forth may be included in "Other" on line 17. Keep your copy of the completed form for your records.

Describe Nature and Extent of Damages

1. CARPETING ❑ Good Condition ❑ Damaged ______
2. DRAPERIES ❑ Good Condition ❑ Damaged ______
3. WINDOWS ❑ Good Condition ❑ Damaged ______
4. WALLS ❑ Good Condition ❑ Damaged ______
5. SCREENS ❑ Good Condition ❑ Damaged ______
6. PAINT ❑ Good Condition ❑ Damaged ______
7. SHELVES ❑ Good Condition ❑ Damaged ______
8. DOORS ❑ Good Condition ❑ Damaged ______
9. PLUMBING FIXTURES ❑ Good Condition ❑ Damaged ______
10. ELECTRICAL FIXTURES ❑ Good Condition ❑ Damaged ______
11. STOVE ❑ Good Condition ❑ Damaged ______
12. REFRIGERATOR ❑ Good Condition ❑ Damaged ______
13. CLOSETS ❑ Good Condition ❑ Damaged ______
14. FURNITURE ❑ Good Condition ❑ Damaged ______
15. CABINETS ❑ Good Condition ❑ Damaged ______
16. FLOORS ❑ Good Condition ❑ Damaged ______
17. OTHER ______

EXTRA INFO

The above is a complete inventory checklist of the premises commonly described as:

Property Address: ______

Commencement Inventory Checklist

(Page 2 of 2)

Inventory checklist made on: ______________________________, 20______

Michigan statute requires that the tenant must furnish the landlord with the tenant's forwarding address within four (4) days after giving up occupancy.

RECEIPT ACKNOWLEDGMENT

I, being the Tenant, hereby acknowledge receipt of two (2) copies of this checklist, which has been provided by Landlord.

_______________________________________ ______________________

Tenant's Signature *Date*

After form is filled out and signed by tenant, return one copy to:

Ralph R. Roberts Real Estate, Inc.
30521 Schoenherr Rd.
Warren, MI 48093

Property Address: ____

Rent Past Due Letter

Send this letter out as soon as a tenant's rent payment is 10 days late.

October 10, 2001

Ronald Renter
999 North Blvd.
Somewhere, USA

Dear Mr. Renter:

As of the writing of this letter, your rent is 10 days late. As you know, rent is due on the first day of the month and we take rent collection very seriously.

Hopefully, this is just an oversight on your part. If that's the case, please send or drop off your rent check immediately—don't forget to add a late charge of $25 as prescribed in your lease—and call my office at 555-1234 to let us know that you have received and acted upon this letter.

If we fail to receive your rent or hear from you by the 25th of the month, we will be forced to protect our interests by taking more drastic measures, including derogatory reports posted to your credit report and even eviction.

Please don't let it come to that. Call us now and resolve this today.

Thank you for your immediate attention to this very critical matter.

Sincerely,

Ralph Roberts

Eviction Pending Letter

This letter should be sent to the tenant as soon as you have decided to move forward with an eviction. The idea is to use a little shock therapy to convince the previously unresponsive renter to move out before the eviction is completed.

Ronald Renter
999 North Blvd.
Somewhere, USA

Mr. Renter:

Since my efforts to contact you about your failure to pay your rent have gone without a response, I have been forced to take drastic measures to ensure that I do not continue to lose money on the property in which you are currently living. If you have not been already, very shortly you will be served by the court with notice of the eviction proceeding I have begun against you.

Physical eviction is the last, and most severe, option available to a landlord. You should know what you will be facing if you choose to allow this to happen. An officer of the court—normally a bailiff—is dispatched to your residence with an eviction team. They enter the house whether or not you are at home. The eviction team begins by placing all small and loose items in garbage bags. This includes everything from the food in the refrigerator and pantry to cherished family photos displayed on the walls and end tables. These garbage bags are hauled out to the curb along with dresser drawers full of personal items, furniture, appliances, and anything else you may own that is in the house. Your bedding is unceremoniously stripped from the mattress and tied into knots to be placed out at the curb with everything else you own.

It's not a pretty scene. But, unfortunately, you have left me with no choice but to move forward with the eviction. Many people in your situation who continue to ignore the situation eventually come home to find their locks changed and everything they own piled up at the curb.

I don't think that either of us wants this to happen. It's up to you. I would much rather solve this problem in a civilized manner, but I have no qualms with using all of the laws and resources at my disposal to protect my interests. Please call me at 555-1234 so we can resolve this situation before you get thrown out on the street.

Sincerely,

Ralph Roberts

Summary

There are plenty of software products, books, and reference materials available to help you create your own leases and rental forms, but the best advice I can offer is: Don't reinvent the wheel. Talk to other investors who have been successful landlords over several years. Ask them what has and hasn't worked for them. See if they will let you have copies of their leases and other rental forms. If you don't know any landlords, join your local property owners association and make use of the resources it provides. Keep in mind, however, it is always a good idea—and well worth the expense—to have a competent local real estate attorney review any legally binding documents before you put them in use.

The forms and contracts you use will have a huge impact on your success as a landlord. Just remember that it is much easier to sort out disagreements when everyone's expectations and responsibilities are clearly laid out at the beginning of the relationship.

SECTION 4

DIVESTING PROPERTY

CHAPTER 19

How and Where to Find Buyers

When the time comes for you to sell a property, there are really two main ways of bringing buyers to the table. One way is to hire a real estate professional to list your house on the local Multiple Listing Service (MLS), which effectively notifies every Realtor in your area that your property is on the market. The other is to try to find a buyer on your own. Of course, you can always apply both methods at the same time, which in my opinion is your best bet. In this chapter, I'll review different marketing techniques that will increase your chances of landing a qualified buyer who is interested in your property.

Realtors and the MLS

With few exceptions, there is no sales tool that is more effective at generating potential real estate buyers than the Multiple Listing Service. While the best real estate agents offer all kinds of value-added services, the MLS remains the trump card that convinces most people to list with them rather than going FSBO (For Sale By Owner). In other words, if an agent does nothing more than simply list your house on the MLS at the exact same price and terms that you seek as a FSBO, it is virtually assured that the Realtor will sell the property more quickly than you can. This is true even if the agent does absolutely no other marketing while you sink time, money, and effort into your marketing.

Just about any real estate agent working with a buyer starts the home search by looking up houses on the MLS, based on the buyer's search criteria. When your property is listed on the MLS, every time a Realtor does a search for a buyer whose specifications match the features of your house, your listing pops up for them to review, which means that you literally have every real estate salesperson in your marketplace working at finding buyers for you. According to some studies, more than 75 percent of all sold listings are sold through the MLS. There is simply no other tool in existence that offers such a concentrated source of buyers.

Why go it alone with a FSBO when such a powerful tool is available to you? Sure, you may be able to save a commission by going it alone—but at what price? How many prime houses will you miss out on buying because you have your money tied up in a property waiting for a buyer? On average, it takes FSBOs double the market time to sell a home that it takes a real estate agent armed with access to the MLS. So instead of simply looking at the size of the commission and using that as the only factor in deciding against a Realtor, figure in all of the costs that will come with doing it yourself. First, you will need a marketing budget, but more important, there will almost certainly be opportunity costs, because with your money tied up in the house you're selling, you won't be able to invest it in other properties. And don't forget about interest expense. How much extra will you pay in interest on your investment capital if it does actually take you twice as long to sell?

There are other perks that come with listing your property with a Realtor. If you hire the same salesperson for each property you sell, the relationship you develop can become a key to your success. The agent can help you check comparable sales prices as you research homes to purchase. Additionally, if the Realtor knows that he will get the listing when you're ready to sell, he will be much more likely to come to you with deals that he uncovers on his own. If you're worried about commission expenses, simply figure the cost of commission into the equation when determining potential expenses on the purchase side of things.

LISTING AGREEMENTS

Real estate agents will usually expect you to sign an "exclusive right-to-sell" listing agreement, which states that if anyone—including you—sells the property during the time of the listing agreement, then the real estate broker is entitled to the commission. For the length of the contract, your agent has guaranteed his or her commission no matter who actually sells the house. Note that when you hire a real estate agent to list and sell your home, you agree upon a commission to be paid when the property sells. That is the only commission that comes out of your pocket. If another agent brings a buyer to the table, it is the responsibility of your agent (the listing agent) to pay the buyer's agent out of his proceeds. There is another type of listing agreement called an "exclusive agency" listing. In this arrangement, you still hire a broker to list and market your property, but that broker earns a commission only if a sale of the house results from his or her efforts. If you unearth the buyer yourself, you pay no commission. This type of listing would be a way to get your home on the MLS and pay a commission only if the MLS or your agent makes the sale. However, it is extremely rare to find agents who will even consider this kind of listing. Your best chance for working out this kind of arrangement is to find a young, aggressive agent who is hungry to put deals together. If you can find a way to make it work, this is an option that could pay off if you invest the time necessary to find the right agent. That way, time and money you put into marketing your house won't be wasted if your connections and effort produce the buyer.

One problem that can arise out of an "exclusive agency" agreement is a dispute over where buyers actually come from. If someone driving by stops to knock on your door and eventually buys the house, who produced the buyer? "Well, I did," you might say. "She stopped here to look at the house and I sold her on it while showing the property." Your agent might then argue, "No, it was my lead. If she hadn't seen my 'For Sale' sign in the front yard, she never would have stopped there." If you do get into this type of arrangement, make sure the details are clearly outlined, especially if you plan on aggressively marketing your home while it's listed. A trip to court to figure out who brought the buyer to the table could quickly cost you much more than the commission you're trying to save.

Your role in securing a buyer

Whether you hire a Realtor or take the For Sale By Owner approach, there are plenty of things you can do on your own to move the property more quickly. Let's take a look at the most effective ones.

Networking

As a real estate investor, one of the best methods for selling your houses is through networking. You should be constantly letting people know that you buy and sell properties; that if they or anyone they know wants to buy or rent a home, they should give you a call. Because you plan on having a regular supply of properties to sell and rent, building your relationships with these contacts is well worth the effort. Some of the people and places where networking will be most effective include

- Friends, family, neighbors, and co-workers
- Other investors you meet through property owners associations, auctions, and doing transactions together
- Nonagent real estate professionals, such as home inspectors, appraisers, and mortgage loan officers

- Maintenance contractors, including roofers, plumbers, electricians, carpenters, etc.
- Tenants and people who live in the neighborhoods surrounding properties you own
- Professionals with whom you regularly interact—e.g., doctors, attorneys, CPAs, stockbrokers, etc.
- Community organizations in which you're active
- Your church
- The market
- The bank
- Anywhere you go and with everyone you meet!

Develop a database of your friends, acquaintances, and other contacts. Then when it comes time to sell or rent a property, you can put together a mailing letting them know what you have available.

Setting effective pricing

If you price your property correctly and let buyers know it's available, it will eventually sell. Pricing may very well be the most critical decision you have to make—and it's totally under your control. Many sellers fall into the trap of saying, "I'll price it a little bit above what I think it's worth and then bring the price down if it doesn't sell." That kind of thinking can cost you big time. You could even miss the market completely.

I've been in real estate for more than 25 years, so I know a little bit about how these things work. Let me explain to you what happens when a house is overpriced. An experienced agent will know you're asking too much right away, so he will use it as a tool to sell another property. He will show his buyers a few homes that are properly priced, and he'll show them yours at the same time. He will take great pains to make sure they see every feature in the other properties that are equal to or better than the features in your house. Then, when he has them back at the office, he'll say something like, "You see how much house you're getting for your money with house A [the properly priced home]. This is a great deal. You get everything house B (your property) has, but at a lower price." Price your property properly and you can use this technique to sell your house by comparing the price to others in the neighborhood.

There are other dangers that come with overpricing. If your house stagnates on the marketplace for an extraordinarily long time without selling, many potential buyers will begin wondering what's wrong with it. They will start looking for flaws that might have scared other potential buyers away. Even if there's nothing wrong with the house, a buyer with a good imagination will find plenty of problems if he or she walks into the door believing your house is saddled with some problem that has kept it from selling.

Overall, my experience has been that homes initially priced at market value sell much more quickly and closer to full market value than those that are overpriced at the start. In addition to the expenses of leaving the property on the market for an extended period of time (interest, opportunity cost, marketing expenses, etc.), a homeowner runs the risk of completely missing the market chasing a falling value.

Picture a solid mature neighborhood that has had pretty stable ownership for 15 to 20 years. Many buyers would love to find a home there, but few people ever sell. Because of that, when a home does go on the market, it is snapped up pretty quickly—usually at or above full price and terms. As this goes on for several years, each seller raises his price accordingly. You get lucky and pick up a property in the neighborhood at a foreclosure auction. (Once you get into foreclosures, you will be surprised at how often solid homes in solid neighborhoods are sold at foreclosure auctions.) You see that similar houses in this subdivision have been selling for about $160,000. What you don't see—or refuse to acknowledge if you do see it—is that prices in this area are artificially high because of the high demand and low supply. Similar homes in a subdivision 15 miles away sell for just $145,000. As long as the demand remains high and the supply low, sellers will continue to get their high asking prices. But as soon as the supply loosens, the property values will settle down to more realistic levels.

Once you get your house, instead of acting quickly to benefit from the high demand, you get a little greedy and decide to see how far you can push the envelope. You set your price at $170,000, figuring you can lower it if the house doesn't sell at that price. While you wait for someone to make an offer on your house, ten families have decided to move and put their homes on the market. (It is not uncommon for ten or more homes to go on the market within a few days of each other in a large subdivision.) When they see the number of available homes in their development, many families decide they want to sell quickly and price their homes accordingly. Suddenly your listing is sitting there at $170,000 while more aggressive owners are listing and selling their homes at $150,000 and $155,000. You reluctantly lower your price to $160,000. Now the couple who lives next door to your house gets divorced and the court orders them to liquidate the marital assets, including their home. The court also decrees that if the property isn't sold within 45 days, it will order it to be auctioned off to the highest bidder. Wanting to avoid an auction at all costs, the couple puts its house on the market at $140,000. Other owners who see this price begin lowering theirs into the high $140s.

Now that the supply of homes in the subdivision has increased, prices have dropped back to their natural levels, and the result is that you will now make about $10,000 to $20,000 less than you would have if you had priced the property correctly in the first place.

What I just described is called "chasing the market," and it happens more often than most people realize.

Consider Creative Financing

Earlier in this book, in the section on property acquisition, I emphasized creative deal making and examined the value of a flexible seller who was willing to consider creative financing. Now that you are the seller, doesn't it make sense that you will have more buyer prospects if you are willing to consider creative financing? I say that you go out and find a buyer who wants the house and then figure out the best way to get him into it. Creative financing is covered more in-depth in the next chapter.

Maintain the Appearance of the Property

The appearance and condition of the property is another sales tool over which you have complete control. When you try to envision what the home should look like in order to sell quickly, think of a builder's model home, where everything is sparkling clean, well organized, bright, and uncluttered. This is how you want your house to look when prospects start driving by and coming to visit. If you will be doing any renovations, choose neutral colors for the walls and carpeting.

Use a "For Sale" Sign in Your Yard

By installing in the front lawn a sign announcing to the world your intention to sell your property, you invoke what I call, "The Rule of 20." Your sign will immediately be noticed by the neighbors in the five houses on either side of yours as well as by those in the ten homes directly across the street from you. Whether you realize it or not, by putting up that sign, you have just created a sales force of 20 or more people. That's because your neighbors and fellow homeowners who live in those 20 homes have a stake in the neighborhood and will quickly begin telling their friends, relatives, and co-workers that a house in their neighborhood is now on the market. And some of the individuals they tell will pass the word on to others. Soon, hundreds of people will know that your house is for sale—just because you decided to install a "For Sale" sign in your yard.

In addition to the word of mouth generated by your neighbors, interest will be generated by any traffic in your neighborhood. You can also use banners and attachments, making the sign a dynamic tool that alerts neighbors and passers-by to open houses, special features, and creative financing options available to buyers. Personally, I think anyone trying to sell a home would be foolish *not* to use a yard sign.

Use House Flyers

A house flyer is a sheet that allows buyers to learn about your property. It should contain photos of the home's interior and exterior; a complete description of the property, the asking price, and available terms; and a contact name and phone number.

House flyers are like miniposters (they can also be like full-size posters, if you want). Only your imagination and creativity can limit the number of places to leave or post them. Here are some ideas:

- Community bulletin boards at restaurants, stores, and churches
- The offices of your doctor and dentist
- Work (This is one place where you should get permission before posting flyers—don't get into trouble with your employer.)
- Local college and university campuses
- Hotels and motels
- The lobbies of apartment complexes
- On the pump at self-serve gas stations
- Anywhere else you go

If you are in doubt whether or not to post or leave a stack of house flyers, go ahead and do it. At worst they might be thrown away. At best, they might unearth the person who buys your property.

A house flyer can be as simple as a typed sheet photocopied along with photos of the property, or as complex as a professionally designed, full-color brochure, but the higher the quality of your flyers, the more effective they will be. If you have a home computer, you should be able to put together an effective house flyer. If at all possible, include color photos. You can do this by having the flyers professionally printed or printing them at home with a color ink-jet printer. The more expensive your house, the more you should spend to have higher quality marketing materials.

Summary

As you can see, when it comes to selling a property quickly, you have a choice between working with an agent and doing it yourself. Clearly there are many benefits to working with an agent, while still taking an active role in finding a buyer for your property. However, if you're determined to sell the property without paying a real estate commission, take a look at my book *Sell It Yourself*. It covers in detail everything I discussed in this chapter and more.

CHAPTER 20

When and How to Sell Your Properties

When you invest in real estate, the profit a deal could eventually yield is determined the day you purchase the property. Much of that profit, however, will never be realized until the day you sell the house. The price and terms of that sale are just as important as the price and terms on the purchase. Do a poor job of structuring the sale and the resulting expenses could suck up all of your profits before the closing ever takes place. This chapter will focus on how to use the terms and timing of your property sales to maximize profit and minimize risk.

Keep a diversified real estate portfolio

When you invest in real estate, you have a number of choices regarding how you can profit from the investment. You can:

- Sell to another investor "as is"
- Make repairs/renovations and flip for a quick sale near market value

- Live there while doing improvements and sell when you buy your next residence
- Turn the house into "no maintenance" monthly income by selling on a lease-option or seller financing
- Hold as a long-term rental property

Personally, I think it's a good idea to strive toward a diversified portfolio of real estate investments. This allows you to go after a larger portion of the pool of homes for sale in your marketplace and permits you some flexibility with properties that don't go according to your initial plans.

For instance, let's say you buy a house with the idea of fixing it and flipping it. During your renovations, however, you discover that the entire heating and cooling system needs to be ripped out and replaced at a cost of four to five thousand dollars. This, and a few other unexpected repairs, throws your entire cost structure out of whack. You quickly realize that if you go ahead with your plan of flipping the property, you will be lucky to break even and will most likely lose some money on the deal. If you're working with a diversified portfolio, you can mentally slide this house into another category. Then, after all of the repairs are done, you can either sell the house for a small loss or rent it for a few years until it appreciates in value enough to sell for a profit—all without hurting your monthly cash flow. You can put a slight premium on the sales price and offer seller financing to the buyer or collect a cash option fee from a tenant-buyer who's willing to sign a lease-option.

Have a sale plan *before* you buy

Even if you make adjustments on the fly once you purchase a property, the time to determine your plan for getting rid of the house should be constructed before you even buy it. Discuss the different sales strategies with your investors so you can convince them to remain as flexible as possible. The more flexible your investors are, the more creative you can become in working through buyers' financing issues.

In working to either sell or rent your property, remember that it's usually better for you to have a deal in place instead of an empty house. The longer you own a property that isn't rented or sold, the more expenses you incur and the less profit you will make. From the moment you own a property—in some cases, even before you own it—you should be working to put a deal together. If a house is undergoing renovations, put a sign in the front yard saying, "If you'd like to buy or rent this house, call 555-1234."

Consider the Bottom Line

When someone expresses interest in buying the house, present an enticing offer. Don't say, "When these repairs are finished, we'll be asking $100,000 for the property." Instead ask, "How much would you be willing to pay for this house?" Or give your potential buyer incentive to move quickly by saying, "You could probably save some money by buying the house as it is now. The only thing is, we'd have to come to an agreement rather quickly because I'm not going to stop the renovations while we negotiate." As you negotiate with prospective buyers, keep in mind what monthly holding expenses the property will present to you. If interest, utilities, and maintenance result in a monthly bill of $1,400, you might consider closing a deal at $97,000 when your initial instincts had been to take no less than $100,000. The months can fly by pretty quickly, and if you flip just two pages of the calendar without selling the house, all of a sudden you're getting only the equivalent of that $97,000 offer, even if someone offers you $100,000.

Whiteboxing

Of course, if you deal with other investors on a regular basis, you might make the decision to let someone else do the renovations and flip the property *as is* for a quick profit. At my company, we prepare homes for sale to other investors through a process called "white-boxing." Whiteboxing is a term I've borrowed from commercial real estate that simply means the house has been prepared for easy and immediate renovation.

The first thing we do is work on the curb appeal. The yard is neatly trimmed and landscaped to make the outside of the house as attractive as possible with little investment. Next, we get the inside of the home ready for renovations. The utilities are turned on and any plumbing or electrical problems are repaired. We clean all windows, install bright bulbs in every light fixture throughout the home, and spray all walls and ceilings with a stain-kill primer. Finally, if the house has a basement, the floors get painted gray or beige.

The whole idea of this process is to make the property attractive to investors and cost-conscious potential owner-occupants. Even though the house needs work—something prospective buyers will know before they visit—it is an attractive investment because its condition allows them to immediately go to work fixing it up without worrying about finding a whole bunch of hidden problems.

Screening prospective buyers

Before you ever agree to a deal and take a property off the market, you should really get a buyer preapproved for financing. This is a check of the buyer's financial situation that determines how much he or she can afford to spend on a house each month. In the good old days, a preapproval letter meant that the buyer was virtually guaranteed to be eligible for the amount of financing outlined in the letter. Unfortunately, as the mortgage industry has gotten more aggressive, preapproval letters have lost a bit of their luster. They can't be counted on quite so much as in the past. Your best bet is to build a relationship with a loan officer and convince him or her to check out all of your potential buyers for you. Most loan officers would be willing to do this for you because each buyer you send to them becomes a prospect for funding whether or not they actually buy your house.

In screening buyers, don't confuse preapproval with prequalification. Despite its flaws, the preapproval process involves actually reviewing financial documents and records before coming to a conclusion about financing. On the other hand, the prequalification process consists of the loan officer asking the buyer questions and then making a determination based on those answers. There is no accounting for the accuracy or completeness of the information that the buyer provides. Either way, it is in your best interests to have your potential buyers talk to someone you know and trust who can give you an unbiased view of their financial picture.

Financing options

Once you gain a grasp of your buyers' money situation and what type of financing they are likely to qualify for, you can determine how to best put the deal together. The following are some details about how to approach the different options that may be available to you in working with a potential buyer. Although some of these options were covered from a buyer's perspective in Chapter 11, when we were reviewing acquisition strategies, here I will be presenting them from a seller's perspective.

MORTGAGE LENDER FINANCING

This is the easiest situation for you. If your buyer gets financing through a lender of some sort, it means that his or her credit and financial situation are good enough to meet any guidelines they may require and that he or she has enough cash to pay a down payment big enough to satisfy the lender's criteria. Some expenses, such as closing costs, remain negotiable, but in essence, you simply have to show up at the closing, deed the house over to its new owners, and collect a check for your proceeds from the sale.

To make a transaction work for the buyer, you may sometimes have to consider doing things such as paying the buyer's closing costs or carrying a seller-held second mortgage on the property. If the buyer closing costs become an issue, you can often work out the problem by raising the purchase price an amount equal to the closing costs and then paying the closing expenses yourself. This nets you out to a zero loss and helps the buyer lower the amount of cash that has to come out of his or her pocket at the closing. You just have to be careful that the amount of money financed does not rise above the appraised value of the property.

A seller-held second mortgage can come into play when your buyer doesn't have funds for a down payment or if his or her lender isn't willing to finance the entire purchase. This is common when your buyer is purchasing the home as an investment property. In that case, lenders typically are willing to fund just 80 percent or less of the purchase price. If the buyer doesn't have the cash necessary to pay the rest at the closing, you can sometimes keep the deal together by agreeing to accept a second mortgage from the buyer covering the shortfall. The buyer then makes regular monthly payments directly to you until the mortgage is paid off. Depending on the amount of the second mortgage, the term of the note is generally not more than five to ten years. This approach is not advisable unless you are confident that the buyer is financially stable and responsible. I recommend that you take a look at his credit report and review his credit history to make sure he is a good credit risk because, quite frankly, if he does default on your mortgage, you aren't likely to be in a very strong position to collect your money. The other way to approach it is to find an investor who purchases second mortgage notes and immediately sell the note off after the closing. Just don't expect to get more than 60 to 70 percent of the mortgage's face value unless the buyer has sterling credit. Conversely, if your buyer's credit is poor, you may be lucky to get even 50 percent of the note's face value from an investor.

Seller Financing

Known by terms such as "land contract" and "trust deed," seller financing is when the seller—in this case, you—acts in place of the bank. An agreement is drawn up, you collect a deposit, and the buyer makes monthly payments directly to you. The deal is amortized in the same manner as an actual mortgage, but it offers you a few advantages a mortgage doesn't. With seller financing, you won't have to take a tax hit on the income all in one year, and you can earn a nice, safe return on the balance owed to you. Additionally, it's not uncommon for buyers to pay a premium and slightly higher interest rate in exchange for getting land contract terms. And in most states, seller-financed homes are much easier to take back when a buyer defaults as opposed to mortgage foreclosures, which can become quite complicated and expensive.

If you build a big enough portfolio of land contracts, it becomes almost like an annuity, with you receiving regular monthly payments without having to do any additional work. Think about it. No matter what you do, that money keeps coming in. And if it ever stops before the land contract is paid off, the debt is secured by the property.

Some investors don't want regular income spread out over 20 or 30 years. They would rather get the income for a few years and then get cashed out of the land contract. There are two ways to do that. The first is to sell the land contract off to another investor. However, just as with seller-held second mortgages, investors will expect to buy the land contract at less than face value. The better the buyer's credit and the longer the land contract has been "seasoned" without delinquent payments, the closer to face value you can expect to earn on the sale. The other way to get cashed out of the land contract down the road is to include a "balloon" payment in the contract. When the balloon comes due (usually in three to five years, but it can be any length you and the buyer agree upon), then the balance of the money owed on the agreement comes due. This allows someone who can't easily get a conventional mortgage to buy a house, establish a solid payment history over the first few years of the contract, and ultimately refinance into a conventional mortgage at or before the balloon date.

Seller financing does have its drawbacks. The most common problem is the "Due on Sale" clause that comes standard in most residential mortgages these days. These clauses state that as soon as you sell the mortgage's underlying property to another person, the bank has the right to demand full payment of the entire remaining balance due on the mortgage note. Since a land contract deal is technically a transfer of title, you absolutely have to consider the consequences of your transaction. If you get your investment capital from an individual, it is much easier to explain the benefits of seller financing. If, however, a financial institution provides your funding and takes a mortgage on each property you purchase, putting together seller financing can become more difficult. My suggestion would be to discuss the seller financing issue with your loan officer when you set up your funding for the purchase of the property. Try to hammer out an agreement that would allow you to sell on a land contract without the bank calling your loan due. If the bank is unwilling to bend on this issue, you can get around it by using lease-options, which I'll discuss in the next section.

Another potential problem with land contracts involves buyers who default on the contract payment. Just as the court system makes it relatively easy to take back a house when the owner doesn't make his or her payments on time, in most places it is normally just as simple for the owner to get current on their payments and reinstate the land contract. A buyer who knows how to play the system can hold on to the property while sapping your time with court battles and hurting your cash flow by not making payments until the court orders him or her to get the account current or risk losing the house.

You can protect yourself somewhat by doing as thorough a credit and reference check as possible and collecting as large a down payment as you can. Also, as with any legally binding document, make sure your attorney prepares it or at least performs a complete review. If you allow a buyer to purchase your property on a no-money-down land contract, you are taking on nearly all of the risk in the transaction. I'm not saying you should never do one of those deals, but I am saying to make sure you know exactly what you're getting into. If you sell to an investor, you can always convince him to put up other property or personal items as security on your deal. If you're creative, you can get the transaction done so everyone is happy and you are in a position to recoup your losses if the buyer defaults.

LEASE-OPTIONS

The subject of lease-options last came up when we talked about them as an acquisition tool that you can use in no-money-down deals. They are even more effective as a way to turn your rental properties into maintenance-free income generators.

A lease-option allows you to gain some of the benefits of the seller-financed sale while avoiding many of the pitfalls. Here are some of the main benefits of selling your property in this manner:

- You avoid the Due on Sale issue because you retain title to the property until the tenant exercises his or her option.
- Because the lease governs the landlord–tenant relationship, getting a nonpaying renter out of the property is accomplished through the relatively simple eviction process instead of the more involved methods required with land contracts and mortgages.
- Because the lease and the option are tied together in the minds of your tenants, they start thinking like homeowners instead of renters. You can even put language in your lease-option that makes the tenant-buyer responsible for all maintenance and repairs. Even if they never exercise their option, they will almost assuredly take better care of your property.
- Instead of collecting a refundable security deposit when your tenants move in, you collect a nonrefundable option fee that is often much larger than the security deposit would have been in the first place.
- The option often allows you to increase your monthly cash flow on the property to a much higher level than you could with a normal renter. When you set up the lease-option, you can build in rent credits that apply part of the monthly rent toward the down payment if the tenant–buyer ever exercises his or her option. These *nonrefundable* credits—up to a few hundred dollars per month depending on the property—are added to the normal monthly rent.

- Like seller financing, you can often add a premium to the sale price of the property.
- You can set up the option so that when it expires, the tenant-buyer can renew it with a cash payment. This hangs a carrot in front of your tenants that keeps them from moving out because of the time and money they have invested in the house and provides you with additional cash flow.

At the end of this chapter, on page 229, you'll find a copy of the option agreement I use in my business. As with all the documents presented in this book, this is intended as a guide only and may not cover all the details of your specific situation. Have your attorney review any of the documents you intend to use.

Equity sharing

Equity-sharing arrangements allow you to sell a property to another person, but keep yourself in the deal as a partner. The idea is that you spread out the risk and share in the profits. I like to use these types of agreements when I have a property that has a decent equity position, yet needs extensive repairs. Instead of hiring a crew to go in and do the renovations, I'll find a handyman-type investor who can handle most of the work on his own. Then I work out a deal with him where he makes the monthly payments necessary to maintain the property and does all of the work required to get it into shape. Then, when we put the finished house back on the market and sell it, we split the profits from the transaction. This arrangement allows me to preserve my cash flow, keep my renovation crew busy on other jobs, and still make a profit on the property. The advantage to your prospective co-owner is that this allows him to get into a deal without needing a huge chunk of money and then convert a little sweat equity into a healthy profit.

As you can see, equity sharing arrangement can be a total win-win situation. However, there is one caveat: Approach equity sharing agreements with caution. Make sure that everything you've agreed upon is in writing. I can tell you from my own experience that the smiles and happy faces on display when you sign an equity-sharing contract can quickly turn into frowns and lawsuits if the language of the agreement is not perfectly clear.

Barter

Barter has been around since humans first stood erect. When cash money wasn't readily available, people still had to figure out a way to transact business. Buying and selling goods and services involved things like trading some chickens for legal work or giving a farmer a cow in exchange for a portion of his harvest. Of course, when money became more widely circulated, bartering faded into the background. Though it still exists in other countries and out-of-the-way places in America much as I have just described, there is also a more high-tech form of barter that could be of use to you as a real estate investor.

Many companies have surplus goods and services that tie up cash that could be used elsewhere. Some of these companies join "Trade Exchanges" which serve as a bank would in providing members with a market, a communications network, and a clearinghouse for bartered transactions. Goods and services are sold by one member to another for a currency called "trade dollars," which have a *cash* value within each exchange. All trade dollars you take in can then be spent on products and services offered by other member companies. At one time or another, I have been a member of all three metro Detroit trade exchanges.

These are big-time organizations. Realize that some trade exchanges are international in scope with thousands of members involved in just about any business you could imagine. People and companies get involved in bartering and trade exchanges because it introduces them to new markets and customers, it allows them to conserve their cash flow, and it serves as an outlet for unused inventory, capacity, or labor. Bartering always picks up in popularity when the economy slows down and cash becomes tighter.

The reason I've told you about all of this is because it's in your best interest to join a trade exchange in your area. Trade dollars are almost as good as cash and having access to a trade exchange could help your cash flow and make a difficult property easier to sell.

If you're a member of a trade exchange, you could agree to accept the down payment—or some portion of the sales price—in trade dollars. You might even find someone willing to sell you property in this way. There's also the option of finding a real estate agent who is willing to accept trade dollars to cover some or all of his/her commissions. Accepting barter allows you to make your property known to an entirely new universe of potential buyers who would not otherwise have been exposed to it. Once you close the deal and get those trade dollars in your account, you can spend them on just about anything. I have spent trade dollars on everything from office supplies, to Detroit Pistons tickets, to dining out, to out-of-town hotel accommodations. Getting involved in barter is a fantastic way to hedge against economic slowdowns when cash is harder to come by.

Like anything else, trade exchanges do have a few drawbacks. There are businesses that mark up products and services they sell on trade. Additionally, especially in good economies, some small companies go "on hold" and stop accepting barter for a time because they have trouble spending the trade dollars they have accumulated. Despite these minor problems, I firmly believe it's well worth your time and effort to check out any trade exchanges located near you.

Summary

As with property acquisition, there are many financial configurations that can be worked out when you are divesting property. By being creative in your approach to working with buyers, you can successfully build a diversified real estate portfolio and realize a handsome return on your investments, even if you stumble on the occasional lemon. Just remember to carefully analyze the arrangements of each deal and to take the time to properly screen buyers and to have a lawyer review any legal agreements you are about to make with potential buyers.

Option to Purchase

This Agreement as made and entered into this *Date* by and between *Sellers* (hereinafter referred to as Sellers) and *Purchaser* (hereinafter referred to as Purchasers).

WHEREAS the purchasers are Tenants in a lease with Sellers of even date herewith of the premises known as *Property Address*.

WHEREAS the parties have agreed to give Purchasers an exclusive option to purchase the leased premises;

NOW THEREFORE, IT IS AGREED AS FOLLOWS:

1. Seller in consideration of the payment of the sum of *Option Fee* and the further consideration that Purchaser is not in default on any of the terms of the Lease Agreement of even date extends to Purchaser the exclusive option to purchase the premises known as *Property Address* for a period of *Number Of Years Of Option* years from the date hereof and subject to the following conditions:
    A. The purchase price is in the amount of *Purchaser Price*. Purchaser and Seller will enter a land contract upon closing of the purchase.
    B. A monthly option fee of *Monthly Option Fee* is received by Seller from Purchaser on or before the first day of each month. This fee will be considered part of the down payment if the option is exercised. If any monthly option payments are not received, this option agreement will be null and void.
    C. Current taxes shall be prorated and adjusted as of the date of closing in accordance with due date. All taxes are considered paid in advance.
    D. Seller will furnish Purchaser with a commitment for title insurance in an amount not less than the purchase price guaranteeing title in the condition required for performance at Purchaser's expense.
2. In the event of the exercise of the option, Purchaser will be given credit toward purchase price of *Option Fee* consideration paid for this option.
3. In order to exercise this option to purchase the Purchaser must send notice in writing to Seller 30 days prior to the date upon which he wishes to exercise the option but in no event later than 30 days prior to the expiration of the option term. Closing on the option will then take place within 10 days of the date that the Title Commitment is furnished to the Purchasers.

4. In the event Purchaser does not exercise his option within the allotted time and provided Purchaser is not in default on any of the terms of the Lease Agreement and in consideration of the payment of the additional sum of $500 on or before *First Years Renewal Date*, the Seller extends to Purchaser a second option to purchase under the same terms and conditions indicated above except that the purchase price for the premises will be *Second Year Purchase Price* for an additional year.
5. In the event of the exercise of the second option to purchase the Purchaser will receive credit towards the purchase price in the amount of *Option Fee* previously paid for the options.
6. In the event Purchaser does not exercise his option within the allotted time and provided that Purchaser is not in default on any of the terms of the Lease Agreement and in consideration of the payment of the additional sum of $500 on or before *Second Years Renewal Date*, the Seller extends to Purchaser a third option of purchase under the same terms and conditions indicated above except that the purchase price for the premises will be *Third Year Purchase Price* for the third year.
7. In the event of the exercise of the third option to purchase the Purchaser will receive credit towards the purchase price in the amount of *Option Fee* previously paid for the options.
8. Seller agrees to renew this option each year for a fee of $500 provided Purchaser is not in default on any of the terms of the Lease Agreement. The renewal date shall be *Month And Day Of Future Renewal Dates* of each year. The purchase price shall increase by three (3%) percent each year. Purchaser shall be responsible for all repairs from the date of this option forward.
9. In the event the Purchasers wish to sell the premises to third parties prior to exercising the option to purchase they may do so provided Purchaser is not in default on any of the terms of the lease of any of the conditions of the option.

DATED THIS: ____________________

WITNESSED BY:

____________________ ____________________

Seller

____________________ ____________________

Purchaser

____

Purchaser

SECTION 5

FINAL THOUGHTS

CHAPTER 21

Real Estate Investing Pitfalls (And How You Can Avoid Them)

This book is filled with tips, techniques, and ideas for making money investing in real estate. Throughout the book I've tried to emphasize the importance of paying close attention to detail and seeking out the advice of experts such as attorneys, appraisers, and other real estate professionals. However, I know from experience that too many investors learn this the hard way, regardless of whatever recommendations and warnings might have been thrown at them before they got started. I believe that the best way to illustrate the importance of being thorough is by sharing a couple of horror stories with you. I hope you can learn from the mistakes of others, and avoid having to make your own.

The cost of impatience

Tom was just getting started buying foreclosures on his own. He had lined up an investor who lent him money and gave him free reign to buy properties at foreclosure auctions. His investor collected back 9.5 percent interest on his money, plus 20 percent of any profit the deal generated. But in exchange for allowing Tom to keep 80 percent of profits, the two had an agreement that Tom would bear the full burden of any losses that his acquisitions might create.

Things started out well. Within two weeks of starting, Tom had already bought two properties—one at a foreclosure auction and a second one for cash from a bank's REO department. Because he lived in a state with no redemption period, Tom was able to take possession of the foreclosure auction property and flip it pretty quickly for a $7,000 profit that he shared with his investor. The second property was undergoing renovations, but also had the look of a winner. Tom couldn't believe how easy it was to make money investing in real estate. He couldn't help calculating numbers to forecast profits. If he continued to buy a property a week with a $7,000 profit per property, he would earn $364,000 for him and his investor. That was more than $291,000 for him alone! Tom was downright giddy.

Not surprisingly, Tom did not keep cruising along at his house-a-week pace. In fact, the opposite happened—all of his prospects seemed to dry up. While the first two deals had practically fallen into his lap one after another, locating the third deal was suddenly harder than finding a needle in a haystack. Nearly a month went by before he came across another property that had even the potential to be a good acquisition. Tom started to doubt himself and began wondering if the foreclosure market could support him.

Finally, Tom unearthed a house he liked. It was an all-brick, four-bedroom, two-car-garage home in one of the better subdivisions in the area. Because the people were still living in the home and they refused to work with him, Tom was forced to come up with a top bid amount without first seeing the inside. No problem, he thought. The house looked to be in good shape on the outside, and the owners had bought it less than two years before for $210,000. And Tom knew the agent who sold it to them. The agent told him that the family had put almost $20,000 worth of improvements and redecorating into the house after they purchased it. After taking all of this into consideration and examining comparable sales in the area, Tom came up with a value of $220,000. After figuring his desired spread and the expenses he anticipated if he actually was the high bidder, Tom came up with a top bid of $178,000. After taking a look at the chain of title, Tom determined that it was indeed the first mortgage that would be sold at the auction. He headed off to the foreclosure sale excited about his chances.

When Tom arrived at the sale, he quickly discovered that he was the only investor considering that property. His heart leaped with excitement. "I'm going to get this one," he told himself. As the substitute trustee began the foreclosure auction by reading some disclosures, something flashed through Tom's mind. "I never checked to see if property taxes are due on this one," he realized with alarm. A little less excited, Tom thought about the 30 to 40 properties he had researched in the past month. "Only one or two owed any back taxes and those were just a few hundred dollars," he reassured himself. "A few hundred bucks won't make a difference on a great house like this," he reasoned. "So my spread drops a little. It's still a great deal."

The substitute trustee looked at Tom. "The bank bids $185,000," he said.

Tom fixed a look of concentration on his face as inner turmoil erupted in his head. "Too high!" Tom's brain screamed. "Let it go! Don't touch this one."

Tom was about to say, "Thanks, but no thanks," when he heard a faint little voice in the back of his head. "Don't let this one slip away," the voice warned. "How long have you waited for this opportunity? What if it's another month before you see another deal?" The voice was growing louder. "So what if your spread gets cut," it continued. "At least you'll be making something. Besides, they just sunk $20,000 into the house. If you just flip it without putting any money into it, you'll make more than $20,000—even at this purchase price. Buy it!" the voice demanded.

"One hundred eighty-five thousand one dollars," Tom finally said with a smile before hustling off to the bank to get the certified funds necessary to pay for the house.

The problems began about ten minutes after Tom left the attorney's office with the deed to the property. Realizing that he still had to check on back taxes, Tom made a phone call.

"Two thousand dollars?" Tom asked incredulously.

"That's just county taxes," the too-pleasant voice responded. "My computer shows that city taxes are also due. You'll have to check with them to find out how much."

Despite a total of $2,500 that he never anticipated being added to his expense list, Tom tried to remain upbeat. He got some good news when he discovered that the family who lost the home had moved out the day of the sale, sparing him the time and cost of an eviction and allowing him to take immediate possession of the property. Tom met his locksmith at the house and anxiously waited to get inside. Peeking through the windows as the lock was picked, Tom convinced himself that the carpeting looked pretty good and hoped that the interior of the home wouldn't need much work.

When the door finally swung open, Tom nearly fell on the floor. The first thing that hit him was the odor. The family obviously had a pet of some sort, judging from the stench of urine. Tom figured it was a large incontinent dog. He quickly realized that the offending odor was in the rug and had probably soaked right through to the pad underneath. The carpeting would have to be ripped out and replaced.

As he walked through the house, the situation only got worse. The few walls that weren't covered with randomly patterned wallpaper were painted dark colors. The master bedroom had a pink ceiling. None of the trim in the home matched. Some rooms had bright white trim while others had various shades of off-white and beige. It became increasingly obvious that the $20,000 the family spent on improvements had been spectacularly misapplied.

Even as he struggled to remain upbeat, Tom realized that in addition to all of the carpeting and wallpaper having to be removed, the entire 2,800-square-foot home would have to be repainted, ceilings and trim included.

Tom immediately started looking for places where he could cut corners and hope to save some of the profit he saw quickly disappearing. A friend recommended a painter who Tom hadn't hired before. According to the friend, this guy worked fast and cheap. You just had to buy the paint and this painter would go into the house and do the work on an hourly basis. Tom's regular painter was working on the REO Tom had purchased a month earlier, so he decided to give this new guy a try. The painter got started on the house and worked at an impressive rate, giving Tom a bit of hope. About halfway through the job, though, the painter disappeared. Two weeks passed with Tom trying to get the painter back on the job or find a replacement painter. When the painter finally reappeared, offering a vague excuse about a family emergency, Tom still didn't have anyone else to complete the job, and reluctantly decided to have this painter wrap things up.

Between supplies, contractors, back taxes, interest, and other expenses, this house was hemorrhaging money and destroying Tom's cash flow. When the house was finally in shape, more than a month after Tom bought it, Tom added up the numbers and was shocked to see that his total expenses had exceeded $20,000. He was into the property for $207,000. He realized that even if he sold it for his full asking price of $220,000, after paying real estate commissions, he would still lose $1,000. He decided against selling it on his own, because at a cost of more than $1,400 a month in interest, he didn't have time to mess around. The final disaster struck as Tom prepared to put the property on the market. When he reviewed comparable listings with his Realtor, Tom discovered that he had overestimated the value of the house. Hoping to improve on the agent's assessment, Tom paid $400 to have a professional appraiser weigh in with his opinion. The appraiser came back with a value of $199,000—even lower than the Realtor's estimate of $205,000.

Tom finally sold the house three months later for $195,000. When all was said and done, he lost more than $15,000 on that one bad deal.

And the Moral Is . . .

The biggest tragedy in this story is that none of it had to happen. Tom's first and biggest mistake was impatience. There were plenty of other errors in Tom's judgment, but impatience was the domino that set the disaster in motion. If Tom had been patient, he never would have bought the property in the first place.

Let's take a look at all of the other mistakes Tom made in this deal and consider how he could have avoided them.

1. Tom put too much stock in the outside appearance of the house. Because he was dying to put a deal together (there's that impatience at work!), Tom convinced himself that because the outside of the house was in such great shape, the inside must be as well. While it is true that outside appearance is normally an indicator of the interior condition, always assume that to be the case when the outside is in bad shape, but NEVER bank on it being true when the outside looks good. Plus, brick holds up much better to neglect than other surfaces, which means that an all-brick exterior can deceive you, as it did Tom.
2. Tom relied on hearsay about the alleged $20,000 in improvements to convince himself that the inside must be in great shape. When you can't see the inside, fully account for any negative things you hear about the inside and don't count on the accuracy of anything positive people tell you about it.
3. Tom obviously didn't scrutinize the comparable sales well enough, since he overpriced the home by $20,000 or more. If you can't get good comparables, or you don't trust your own pricing ability, ask a Realtor to help you. Let her know that if she helps you with pricing, she will get the listing on anything you buy and flip. As you consider comparable sales, keep in mind that in higher-end neighborhoods certain floor plans and extra amenities will have a big impact on a home's value, and carefully consider how the property you're considering stacks up when it comes to those extras.

4. Tom's professional appraisal came way too late. If he had gotten the appraisal before the sale, do you think he still would have bought that home at $185,000? Even if you can't get inside a house before the sale, you can buy what's called a "drive-by" appraisal for a few hundred bucks. Ask the appraiser to give you a value based on the outside appearance, assuming that the inside is in perfect condition, since it should be once you finish repairs and renovations. Of course, this type of appraisal would only determine what you can expect the house to sell for. If you are using it as a guide for figuring a potential purchase price, keep in mind that the appraisal assumes the inside is in great condition and doesn't factor in interest, taxes, repairs, or other expenses.
5. Tom's research was incomplete. He went to the foreclosure auction without checking for back taxes. If he had done that, he wouldn't have purchased that house. I guarantee you that the one time you fail to check something in your research, your lack of preparation will jump up and bite you in the wallet. There are already too many unknowns in this kind of transaction—and that's why you have to lay your hands on as much of the known information as possible.
6. The excitement of the sale and the overwhelming desire to do a deal caused Tom to break the cardinal rule of auctions: Don't EVER raise your bid above your predetermined top bid. It's just not worth the risk. If you find that you're losing out on properties because your top bid is consistently too low, examine your process for determining that price and apply any adjustments to the next property. Don't make adjustments on the fly. Use your research to come up with a top bid and then stick with it!
7. When Tom started mentally cutting his spread in an effort to convince himself to buy the property, all he could do was hope that he wouldn't have to repaint and replace the carpeting, because then his spread would disappear for sure. When you can't get inside a house, always assume that it will need new paint

and carpet throughout and adjust your top bid accordingly. This is especially important when you buy larger, higher-end homes.

8. Hiring an untested painter at an hourly rate for such a big job was a mistake. In the long run, you will be better off collecting bids for each job from several contractors before awarding the contract to one of them. Have them tell you what the job will cost, and then hold them to that price. And make sure any worker you hire comes with solid recommendation from someone you trust. If you must hire an hourly worker, or one without a strong recommendation, start him off with a smaller job so you can get a feel for his work ethic and the quality of his work.
9. Tom underestimated his interest expenses. Having his painter disappear for two weeks didn't help matters, either. The more you spend on a property, the more interest expenses are likely to eat into your spread. Before you buy a house, find out what the average market time is in your area for that type of home. Add to that the amount of time you expect to spend on renovations and at least another month's cushion. If the market has been slowing down, add two or three months. Figure out what your interest expense will be for that length of time and work the numbers into your calculations of a top bid price.

Fortunately for Tom, while this transaction was certainly a setback, it did not ground his whole operation. He was able to overcome and learn from his mistakes and become a more successful investor because of the experience.

Another costly lesson

I have always been a big believer in the value of labor-saving tools and systems. Over the years, as I've done more and more deals, I've tried to develop forms and checklists that cover repetitive tasks. This accomplishes two things. First, it keeps important details from slipping through the cracks, because if something is written down on paper and I refer to it every time I repeat a procedure, such as buying a property, it's highly unlikely that I will forget to do it. Second, these systems allow me to entrust repetitive tasks to assistants without need for extended training. That way, I can focus my energies on the money-producing job of finding deals.

A few years ago, I thought I had great systems in place and I knew that my staff was very competent. In my opinion, we had a fine-tuned operation that rolled through transactions without any major problems. Whatever small problems did arise, my staff normally handled them before I even learned about them. You might say that I grew a little complacent and maybe even a little cocky. I'm sure you can figure out by now that something went horribly wrong. Let's just say that fate has a way of putting in their place those people who grow a bit too overconfident.

It started out like so many other days. I got up, showered and dressed, and had breakfast with my kids before heading to the office. I was looking forward to a great morning. We had closed on a nice little cash purchase property just the day before. It was a two-bedroom home that we bought for a little less than $35,000 and didn't anticipate putting more than another $5,000 into, and it would be worth about $60,000 when repairs were completed. It was about as close to a sure thing as you can get in this business.

As I walked into our building, I quickly felt an undercurrent of stress running through the office—a different type of stress than what normally comes with a fast-paced workplace. Something was going on and I decided to find out what it was. I found one of my top assistants in her office on the verge of tears.

"What's the matter," I asked.

"The house we closed on yesterday burned down last night," she finally confessed after a bit more prodding from me.

I was a bit shaken by the news but tried to appear calm. "That's okay," I said. "It's nothing to cry about. Things like this happen. Just call the insurance company and have them get started on our claim."

She sat there with her head in her hands and refused to look at me.

"What?" I asked. "What else is wrong?"

"Well, Ralph," she eventually began in a timid voice. "We forgot . . ." her voice trailed off.

"We forgot what?" I asked, my blood pressure rising as I anticipated her answer.

"Insurance," she barely whispered.

"We forgot to get insurance?" I asked in disbelief.

She slowly shook her head in affirmation.

A few hours later—after I had managed to calm myself down—I called together all of the people who had worked on that file to see where the breakdown had occurred. Four people had been involved in that transaction, myself included, and everyone figured that someone else would take care of the insurance.

The first thing we did after the meeting was to check all of our other properties to make sure that everything else was insured. Second, we immediately reviewed our forms and checklist, and not surprisingly at this point, discovered that nowhere in the whole system was there a written reminder to order insurance on a property. It was just something that someone had always done. We immediately revised our system so that it included a reminder, in large print, to order insurance immediately upon a seller's acceptance of our offer. Finally, I got together with my key people so we could look closely at the system and make sure that there weren't any other important things not included in writing.

The danger of leaving your own backyard

As we discussed earlier in the book, I love to lend hard money to other investors through my mortgage company and I've done it successfully for quite a few years in metro Detroit. Additionally, because of the points and interest rate involved, hard money lending can be lucrative for the loan officer as well as the lender. That is why I naturally have a fair amount of skepticism when a loan officer brings me an unfamiliar investor seeking hard money. It's not so much that I think the loan officer would intentionally misrepresent anything, but with a large commission hanging in the balance, it is easy for him or her to be unrealistically optimistic and biased when presenting a potential deal.

Needless to say, my radar was up when one of my better loan officers brought me an investor seeking financing for 20 properties in Muskegon, a Michigan city more than fours hours away by car. My skepticism was gradually broken down, though, as I met the buyer and his real estate agent. The deal looked even more favorable when I saw photos and appraisals of the properties. Even though I had no personal knowledge of the Muskegon marketplace, the people I met and the documents they produced convinced me to loan out the money.

Thankfully, we decided to get them started with funding for just three of the properties. The appraisals showed that these homes would be worth $60,000, $70,000, and $80,000 once renovations were complete. Based on those appraisals, we loaned out a total of $140,000 with the promise of another $600,000 to $900,000 for the other 17 properties if things went well.

Obviously, I wouldn't be telling this story now unless something had gone wrong with the deal. As we prepared to close on the other 17 loans, I decided to take a ride to Muskegon to check things out. After driving four hours, I discovered I'd been duped by all of the Muskegon people who had conspired to defraud me. In reality, all 20 properties—including the three we'd already funded—were run-down, boarded-up, and in some cases condemned properties that this ring of people had purchased for less than $20,000 apiece. There's no way these houses will ever be worth the amounts shown in the appraisals.

We immediately called off the other loan closings and began examining our legal options. When the loan payments stopped coming in, we were forced to take the properties back through foreclosure. Now I own three houses on the other side of the state that are worth a total of just $70,000, meaning we've already lost at least $70,000 on the deal.

The group that fooled me was quite organized and ingenious. Before taking photos of the subject properties, they cleaned up the yards, pulled boards off the windows, parked cars in the driveways, and generally made the homes look inhabited. They slipped the appraiser a few hundred bucks to falsify information on the appraisals. They found an individual with relatively good credit scores who knew next to nothing about real estate (so he wouldn't question the legality of their plan) and convinced him to join them.

Despite all their efforts, I still could have easily avoided this whole mess. This deal went down because my success had caused my ego to grow to the point where I believed I could do deals in other markets without even visiting them. If a similar group of loans from one of the three counties I work in metro Detroit had come before me, it never would have had a prayer of getting funded. That's because I know my marketplace inside and out. I was blinded by dollar signs and tried to stretch myself to an area I didn't really know, and it wound up biting me in the backside. In addition to losing money on the deal, I now have to spend even more time and money cleaning up a mess on the other side of the state instead of devoting those same resources to making money here in the marketplace I know best.

This whole experience hammered home the lesson that you will be most successful in real estate when you do it in your own backyard. You need to have personal access to a property and first-hand knowledge of the marketplace before putting your money at risk. If I would have simply visited Muskegon before doing the first three loans, I could have nipped this thing in the bud.

Summary

The road to success in real estate investing can be a bumpy one; however, with a little caution, common sense, and lots of careful preparation, many of those bumps can be avoided. The upside is that, as long as it doesn't ruin your venture, there is always a lesson to be learned from a mistake. But the best kind of mistake to learn from is one made by someone else. Tom paid $15,000 for his lesson and I paid $35,000 for mine. Take the time you need to avoid such costly lessons.

Real Estate *Can* Make You Rich

Now that I've scared you into exercising caution, let me close on a positive note by sharing with you a few success stories to show how rewarding investing in real estate can be.

All signs said "No Deal," but perseverance paid off

My co-author, Joe Hafner, applies many of the techniques we've discussed in this book in his real estate investment operation in and around Nashville, Tennessee. This first story is about a foreclosure deal he recently put together.

Joe regularly researched every single property contained in the foreclosure listings in Rutherford County, southeast of Nashville. That adds up to about 30 to 40 properties per month that he checks out at the Register of Deeds office and drives by to examine in person. When he came across this particular house, it certainly didn't jump out at him as a potentially great deal. Actually, just the opposite was true. It had several strikes against it as a potential foreclosure auction purchase.

First of all, the property was on the low end of the price range for the marketplace, and it had been purchased less than a year earlier. Joe's experience was that the majority of these types of homes were bought with little money down. In fact, he had yet to come across a solid deal on a foreclosure property in this price range where the deed date was less than four years before the auction date. And this property's deed date was less than a year ago. Even though his instinct was to forget about the house, Joe continued his research.

Joe discovered that the house was listed on the MLS and an offer was pending. This was a sure sign that the property would never make it to the foreclosure auction. The owners had obviously decided to sell the house rather than lose it, and the pending status meant that they had received and accepted an offer from a purchaser. It was only a matter of getting the deal closed now.

Nevertheless, even with these two huge strikes against a potential deal, Joe continued his research. After all, he was already checking out other properties, and spending a few minutes on this one wasn't a significant drain on his time.

After completing his research and examining the property, Joe was presented with a dilemma. The floor plan of the house was one common in his area and included an expandable upstairs. If the expansion were complete, the house would be worth about $115,000. If the expansion were not completed—meaning that the upstairs was just attic space—the property would be worth about $103,000. Wanting to err on the side of caution, Joe assumed that the house was not expanded and set the value at $103,000 and, based on that price, determined that he could afford to bid up to $78,000. Figuring that the closing of the pending deal would cause the auction to be canceled, Joe then forgot about that particular property until the day it was scheduled to hit the auction block.

On the morning of the scheduled sale date, Joe called the substitute trustee to ask about the house and was surprised to discover that it was still scheduled to go to sale. With nothing to lose, he then called both real estate agents who had been involved in the pending sale to find out if maybe the sale would close that day. Both agents knew about the foreclosure and both assumed that their deal on the house was dead. The seller had failed to show up for three different closing dates. Having never seen the inside of the house, Joe asked some questions and found out from both agents that the upstairs was indeed finished. Then he asked the buyer's agent if his clients still wanted the property. The agent said that his buyers definitely wanted the house and faxed Joe a copy of the purchase agreement showing that they had agreed to pay $110,500 for the property.

Knowing that the expansion was complete, Joe could afford to raise his top bid up to $87,000. When he arrived at the foreclosure sale, Joe was not surprised to discover that no other investors were on hand to bid on the property. They were probably turned off by the strikes against the deal that had tempted Joe to give up on it as well. It turned out that when the owner had originally bought the house, the bank that provided the financing had required him to put down a large down payment because of concerns that he might abandon the property and leave the country without notice. Sure enough, that was exactly what he had done. So when the bank made its opening bid of $86,729.48, Joe wasted no time in outbidding them, and he purchased the house for $86,730.

Once he had the deed in hand, he immediately called the two agents and told them that if the buyers were still willing, he would sell them the house at the exact same price and terms—including full commissions for both agents—they had agreed upon with the previous owner. Three days later, Joe walked out of the closing with a check for $100,626.52. After paying back the purchase price, a profit of just under $14,000 was left over for Joe. Not bad for a deal that looked as if it had no chance of happening.

Joe's perseverance was clearly an asset in this deal. It didn't take a lot of extra time for Joe to continue following up on this deal, and the payoff was well worth the time and effort he put into it.

Hitting the jackpot with nonperforming paper

My staff works on cash acquisitions, foreclosures, and paper deals. They recently put together one of the better paper deals my company has produced.

John (not his real name) owned a large home on a lake in one of the richest counties in the entire country—Oakland County, Michigan. His home was worth about $480,000. But the property was encumbered with liens totaling more than $520,000. When John's business ran into some problems, he was left in a real bind. He could no longer afford the monthly payments on his home, but he couldn't sell it either. Even if someone had offered the full appraised value of $480,000, he still would have needed to come up with more than $40,000 to pay off the rest of the liens. Because my staff regularly track all of the foreclosures in Oakland County, they eventually came across John's house and quickly realized that it would make an excellent purchase. The primary mortgage was going to foreclosure auction for $252,000. Looking at all of the other liens, we became relatively certain that John would be unable to redeem the house during the six-month redemption period that would follow the sale. The only problem was that we didn't really want to tie up a quarter million dollars of investment capital on a single home for half a year if we didn't have to.

My team contacted John and explained to him our intention of buying his home at the foreclosure auction. We also explained that we would prefer to work with him to create a win-win deal for both John and our company rather than wait for the redemption period to expire. John, who had few options left, agreed to see what we could work out.

In addition to the $252,000 first lien, there were three junior mortgages held by two different banks totaling more than $110,000, along with three state tax and IRS liens worth almost $160,000.

When the foreclosure auction arrived, we paid off the primary lien, received a Sheriff's Deed, and the clock began ticking. Because we had forced ourselves into the middle of the transaction by purchasing the lien, John now had little choice but to work with us. And all of the pressure to put the deal together was on him. In six months, we would own the home and he would get nothing.

My staff immediately began negotiating with the two financial institutions that held junior notes. Remember, the clock was ticking on those banks too. They either had to pay off the first lien, work out some other sort of deal, or face losing their position as well. We eventually worked out a deal where the junior mortgage holders agreed to release their liens from the property for a total payment of $58,000—a discount of nearly 50 percent.

At the same time, we were also working on the IRS and state tax liens. Things moved much more slowly there. Fortunately, over the years I have developed a relationship with a former IRS investigator who knows the tax codes inside out. I brought him in to consult with us on the deal. He confirmed that because the liens were levied against John as an individual, while both John's and his wife's names were on the title to the property, the IRS was not allowed to dilute John's wife's interest in the home by putting the lien against only John on the property. With my consultant's help we managed to get both IRS liens and the Michigan state tax lien completely removed from the title.

Once all of these negotiations were complete, we put the house up for sale at a price below market value. A month or so later, we sold the property to a cash buyer for $430,000. John and his wife received more than $60,000 in proceeds and my company earned almost $50,000 on the deal, plus the commission we earned as the listing agent in the transaction. The entire deal took nearly four months to complete, but the results—more than $60,000 in profits earned by my company—were well worth the time and effort.

Summary

Being thorough and keeping after your research even after a potential deal seems unlikely to take place can pay off huge, as was the case in the preceding stories. Of course, not every deal you'll make will be as profitable as the two I just recounted, but just one or two transactions like this each year would make a huge difference in your real estate portfolio. And just think what profits like this can mean over the long run. Not only will they mean extra cash for life's necessities and luxuries, but, more important, they will provide you with cash flow that you can put into other real estate deals, accelerating the rate at which you'll build the kind of portfolio you want. With perseverance, you can edge out the competition again and again, finding diamonds in the rough from which you can reap real wealth.

ABOUT THE AUTHORS

Ralph Roberts bought his first house more than 20 years ago at the age of 19. Since then, he has consistently demonstrated an uncanny knack for closing the deal. For nearly a decade he has closed the deal on an average of more than 600 residential real estate transactions annually. In comparison, agents at the top 250 residential real estate firms in the USA sell an average of 11 homes per year-or 54 times less than Ralph. Such prolific numbers have prompted positive attention from CNN, Fox News Channel, the *Associated Press*, CNBC, *MONEY*, *Wealth*, *Fast Company*, *Success*, and *TIME* magazine, which called him, "the best-selling Realtor in America."

Ralph is so good at what he does that salespeople and real estate investors from around the world pay for the opportunity to "shadow" him so they can learn about the methods Ralph has used to rise to the top and remain there. A popular lecturer and motivational speaker, Ralph's other books include *Walk Like a Giant, Sell Like a Madman; 52 Weeks of Sales Success; and Sell It Yourself.*

Ralph can be reached at Ralph R. Roberts Real Estate, Inc., 30521 Schoenherr, Warren, MI 48093, or by email at ralph@ralphroberts.com.

Joe Hafner is a writer and entrepreneur based in Murfreesboro, Tennessee. During his tenure with Ralph R. Roberts Real Estate, Inc., Joe headed up the company's marketing, sales training, and foreclosure investment divisions. His background includes experience in public relations, marketing, sales, and the toy and game industry.

The co-founder of TM Entertainment, Inc., Joe was a member of the team that invented several award-winning card games, including The Game of HotSeat, and Quoz, which was recently named one of *Game* magazine's Top 100 games.

The co-author of *Sell It Yourself*, Joe recently completed his first novel.

Using many of the principles and methods described in this book, he has founded and refined a successful real estate investment operation based in Middle Tennessee.

INDEX

Page numbers in italics refer to illustrations and tables.

B

C

D

G

H

I

J

K

L

M